Growing Up in the Care of Strangers

Growing Up in the Care of Strangers

The Experiences, Insights and Recommendations
of Eleven Former Foster Kids

Compiled and Edited by

Waln K. Brown, Ph.D.
and
John R. Seita, Ed.D.

William Gladden Foundation Press

TALLAHASSEE   BATTLE CREEK

Growing Up in the Care of Strangers
The Experiences, Insights & Recommendations of Eleven Former
Foster Kids edited by Waln K. Brown and John R. Seita

William Gladden Foundation Press
2804 Cavan Drive
Tallahassee, FL 32309-3219
(850) 668-8574

walnbrown@comcast.net
orders@williamgladdenfoundation.org
http://www.williamgladdenfoundation.org

ISBN 978-0-9824510-0-7

Library of Congress Cataloging-in-Publication Data
Brown, Waln and John Seita
Growing Up in the Care of Strangers: The Experiences, Insights &
Recommendations of Eleven Former Foster Kids, edited by Waln K.
Brown and John R. Seita

Library of Congress Control Number: 2009927375

Printed in the United States of America

First Printing, August 2009
Second Printing, October 2009

Contents

Preface

Growing up in placement takes a toll, not just on the children and adolescents but also on the professionals charged with their care. Judges, policy makers, administrators, probation officers, psychiatrists, psychologists, counselors, caseworkers, social workers, foster parents, house parents, guardians ad litem, CASA volunteers, child welfare advocates, educators and program staff make critical decisions that can affect a child's life forever. The more attuned they are to what helps or hinders the development of these vulnerable young people, the more likely they are to make the appropriate decisions required to promote positive placement experiences and healthy adult outcomes.

The purpose of this book is to provide child welfare professionals insightful feedback from former foster children who grew up in juvenile justice, foster care, orphanage, adoptive and mental health placements. What makes this book particularly instructive derives from the authors' credentials. They are college-educated adults who masterfully intertwine their childhood stories with mature perspective and their own professional expertise.

The other audiences this book hopes to reach include youth in placement and students who plan to enter careers in child welfare. Children currently in care need to know that others have experienced childhoods as bad as or worse than their own, that they survived and how they did it. Students preparing to work with troubled or dependent young people should learn about a side of life they probably have not experienced before they make decisions that may adversely affect these at-risk youth. Sometimes a wide abyss separates theory and reality.

Acknowledgements

An idiom advises, "Never judge a book by its cover." With respect to this book cover, however, precisely the opposite is true. The haunting image of a lost child moving her or his meager belongings from one placement to the next captures the essence of the life stories herein recounted, a pictorial metaphor shared by millions of foster children raised in the care of strangers.

Famed watercolorist Thomas A. Newnam married his artistic talent with years of experience as a juvenile probation officer and family therapist to create the snapshot of a foster child in transition that tantalized you to explore beyond the cover art into the spirit of this book. Tom has an uncanny genius for reinforcing the phrase that promises, "A picture is worth a thousand words." Visit his website at www.sageandbrush.com and learn why. Not to be outdone, Tom's brother, Randy Newnam, turned the cover art into a PDF file and applied his vast publishing, marketing and advertising experience to frame Tom's cover art. Thank you both for sharing your gifts.

Prologue

Revealing one's deepest, darkest, most painful experiences is no easy task. Doing so requires re-opening psychological wounds and unlocking painful memories banished long ago to the secret dungeons of the mind. This is certainly true for the authors of the stories in this book, most of whom suffered dangerous and dysfunctional childhoods requiring removal from their families and placement in out-of-home care. They have chosen to reflect on their childhood experiences through the lens of adult professionals, so that their unique knowledge might reach receptive minds looking to improve services to today's youth. Their pre-placement remembrances may shock you. Their in-placement experiences may alarm you. Their post-placement adaptations may inspire you. Most of all, their insights and recommendations may enlighten you, and that is the mission of this book.

Admittedly, the authors of these stories do not represent a random sample of children who spent time in out-of-home care. We purposely sought out college-educated professionals who were willing to do the hard work required to delve into their memories of childhood and put their painful remembrances and recommendations for change on paper so that others might learn from their lifetime of experiences. However, we did seek diversity as regards type of placement, gender, race and age. Therefore, the authors represent the gamut of placement experiences other than substance abuse, including juvenile justice, mental health, adoptive, orphanage and foster care. Three of the 11 authors hold bachelor's degrees. Eight have postgraduate degrees. They are white and black, male and female and range in age from their mid-20s to late-60s.

The 40-year span from the youngest to the oldest author gives these stories a unique perspective because so much happened in children's social services over the four decades of placement experiences these authors represent. The de-institutionalization movement of the 1970s, for example, supplanted orphanages with foster homes. Several of the authors lived in institutional care before or during this radical paradigm shift. Their experiences and recommendations, compared to the post-de-institutionalization authors who mostly experienced foster care, is particularly thought-provoking.

The authors also differentiate themselves from the norm by the depth and breadth of their professional expertise. For example, more than half worked directly with children in care at some point in their careers. Others hold administrative positions in programs for children in placement. Some conduct research about youth-at-risk issues and contribute to the literature by writing books, scholarly articles and popular publications. A few teach or mentor social work students. Many train and educate children's services professionals. All remain deeply committed to advancing the quality of care for this vulnerable group of children whose welfare rests with people who have not experienced the potentially devastating effects of removal from their families and growing up in the care of strangers.

Abuse, neglect, parental death and acute family dysfunction typify the reasons why the authors required out-of-home care. Most of them lived in multiple placements, as many as 17. Over half experienced several types of placement, such as foster homes, orphanages, juvenile detention centers or mental health facilities. The majority spent all or most of their time in foster care placements, including foster families, kinship care and group homes. Some of their placement experiences turned out well; others did not. It is toward providing an understanding of what placements and services they believe are in "the best interests of the child" that the authors have opened up their lives to inspection.

This memorial is dedicated to the children
in the care of strangers,
and to the strangers who care
for these girls and boys.
Like candles in the wind on a stormy night,
some cling desperately to a flickering life;
others succumb to its overwhelming force;
while still others possess the wick,
burning defiantly with purpose,
refusing extinguishment.
Their gift to each other and to us
is a light in the storm
—however dim—
to mark the path of a hopeful life fulfilled.

–Phil E. Quinn

Confessions of an Ex-Juvenile Delinquent

‎⊰◊⊱

WALN BROWN

It seemed like the whole world was against me, and at such a young age, I was too immature to make heads or tails of it. All I knew was that I hurt, deeply. My emotions and behaviors increasingly reflected the turmoil that occupied my troubled mind.

The fights between Mom and Dad started it all. They yelled and fought with each other for as far back as I could remember. I did not know why they were so mad at each other. What I did know was that their fighting hurt and confused me. I knew they no longer loved each other, and I was scared they no longer loved me either. The years of fighting ate away at my emotions, slowly but steadily, like dripping battery acid.

Dad finally left us for the last time when I was 11. At first, things were not too bad. At least there were no more fights. I visited Dad every Sunday. We did fun things that dads do with their sons: fish, play catch, go bowling. We could still be together. Sadly, though, that joy did not last long. Sunday soon became a day of pain. Mom said bad things about Dad before and after the visits. Dad said mean things about Mom during the visits. I was caught somewhere in the middle of their war. Their words tore me apart, like two mad dogs ripping a carcass in half. It was as if one wanted me to hate the other, but I wanted to love them both, to share their lives.

Mom always bathed me in her "crazy clean" solution of Lysol and ammonia when I returned from visiting Dad. She said he was a "dirty man," and she would not allow his filthy germs in our house, although technically, it was Nanan and Grandad's tiny house where we went to live after Dad abandoned us.

The Sunday visits with Dad dragged on. Each visit grew more difficult as Mom and Dad fought through me. My guts felt like broken glass. My brain would not think past the pain. I was dying inside. That is why I tried to kill myself. Sleeping pills seemed like the best way to end it all. The doctors pumped the pills from my stomach, forcing me to live, but I no longer felt alive anymore. I had lost my daddy, after all, and I could not comprehend why. Was it my fault?

The Sunday visits with Dad eventually came to an abrupt halt, but it was not the war between Mom and Dad that killed our visits. On that fateful final Sunday, Dad had another boy with him. He hugged the boy close to him, as fathers do with sons they love. He never hugged me. Dad told me how he planned to marry the boy's mother and make the boy his son. That was our last visit. I could see that Dad no longer loved me, that the other boy had taken my place.

My life crashed after that. Painful questions, uncertainties and guilt feelings consumed my thoughts. Why did Dad trade me for another son? Why did Mom act so strangely? Did I cause their divorce? What would become of us? I became a nervous wreck. My body shook and twitched. Pimples erupted like volcanoes all over my face and upper torso. My clothes reeked of "crazy clean" solution. People joked about how I looked and smelled. I felt ugly and unwanted. My brain kept going around and around in circles, searching for answers to questions that defied my immature understanding. I almost failed seventh grade.

Mom was always upset with me. We began to fight like she and Dad had. Sometimes she compared me to him, but never in good ways. I received the blame for everything. We could not talk without arguing. That is why I began running with a gang. I spent more and more time on the streets. On the streets, we kids were in charge. The streets let us escape from the problems at school and at home. Home was just a place to eat, sleep and catch heck.

Mom put me in the Tressler Lutheran Home for orphaned, neglected and dependent children that summer. There were a couple hundred boys and girls there. They were orphans or kids like me whose parents did not know what to do with them. I cried day-in and day-out. I could not understand why both Dad and Mom had gotten rid of me. Was I that terrible of a son that even my own mother and father did not love me or want me?

Mom took me back, but it was not her idea. The people at the Home told her there was nothing they could do for me. They said I was "antisocial," and that I was "not taking advantage of the program." Even the orphanage did not want me. Everybody, even the people whose job it was to take care of kids like me, saw me as worthless.

Home became even more of a pain. Mom and I grew further apart. She did not know what to do with me. I no longer trusted her. We fought or did not talk at all. There was no joy in our house, just emotional sickness eating away at our minds.

School was no better. I began the eighth grade in a special education class. Most of my classmates were older. A few could not read or write. Some were in gangs. Teachers and other students called us "hoods" and "troublemakers." I soon fit in. These were my people, outcasts, losers, failures, the unwanted students who did not fit elsewhere, the square pegs.

Halfway through eighth grade, the school decided to promote me to a higher academic class. My grades dropped like a stone. I barely passed the year.

Ninth grade was even worse. They put me in the College Preparatory curriculum. Subjects like Latin and algebra were way beyond my ability to concentrate. My mind was not on conjugating verbs or solving equations; it was busy trying to comprehend what was happening to my family and to me. Soon, I was failing nearly every class.

My social life was no better. The other students called me "dumb" and treated me like dirt. The teachers made me feel foolish. I was always serving detention for some behavioral problem, such as chewing gum or forgetting my homework or talking back. I knew I would flunk the year. I did not care. I did not care about anything.

The second year in ninth grade was no better than the first. The other students knew I had failed the grade. The teachers threw me out of class, hit or slapped me or gave me detention for breaking one rule or another. The principal reported my social and academic indiscretions to Mom. I was on everybody's list of troublemakers.

Fighting was what really got me into trouble. I was tired of people shoving me around or making me feel foolish. If someone tried to hurt me, then I would hurt him back: pain for pain. If you harm me, then I will harm you too. Maybe that way people would stop mistreating me, my confused and immature mind reasoned.

One lunch period, another student started messing with me. "So, I hear you think you're a tough guy," he sneered. I faked as if I did not hear him. That made him very mad. He took a swing at me, hitting me squarely on a sore pimple. The world turned red and pain short-circuited my body. The fight was on. Back and forth, we wrestled. I squeezed his neck between my hands, beating his head against a wooden door that resounded like the crack of thunder with each blow. All the anger inside me flowed onto him. Soon he was unconscious, a bloody mess lying limp on the marble floor.

They carried him to the nurse. I was marched to the principal's office, a place with which I had become quite familiar. The principal did not listen to my side of the story. He just threw me out of school. He said that I "had it coming." Then he called the York County (PA) Juvenile Probation Office.

I was in real trouble this time. Since school expelled me, they put me in the juvenile detention center, locked away inside a chicken wire cage for eleven days until a judge heard my case.

The judge listened to the principal, the probation officer and Mom. They told him about my history of problems at school and at home. Then he asked me why I was in so much trouble. I tried telling him about my rotten life, but I could not put into words what my confused mind could not comprehend. He adjudicated me a delinquent child and placed me on juvenile probation.

Every week I met with the probation officer. He knew about everything I did because the school principal and Mom told him. I felt as if I were a criminal. The whole world kept closing in on me.

It was just before the end of ninth grade that something inside my head finally snapped. I had just begun taking a new anti-zit drug, which made me weak and light-headed, kind of like tripping, I guess. Mom and I were having one of our arguments. I could take no more. I ran from the house screaming that I wanted to die. I ran as fast and as far as my legs would carry me. Then I hid in the woods until the sun went down. When it got dark, I went home and fell asleep on the back porch. Where else could I go?

Mom found me and called the cops. They escorted me to their patrol car and then drove me to a hospital. I was too tired to fight back.

After I got to the hospital, I threw a fit. Someone screamed. A nurse came toward me. I kicked at her. Someone else screamed. Men dressed in white grabbed me and pinned me down. A long needle shot something deep into my arm. The lights went out.

In the nightmare that followed that moment of blackout, and revisited me for years thereafter, I am looking down at myself from the heavens. I see myself balled up on the floor in the corner of an empty white room. A lone light bulb hanging from a frayed brown wire, my sole companion, lights my antiseptic white universe. I'm crying out for somebody to save me but I'm alone, so very alone. Somebody help me, please! I'm over here! Don't you see me? Can't you hear me? I'm still here. See? While I am screaming, my body is shrinking. I'm getting smaller and smaller. I keep crying out and shrinking into the corner until there is nothing left of me but the tiniest dot where the straight lines of the two walls meet the floor. Only the faintest sound of my voice remains. Then it, too, is gone.

When I woke up, I was in a small white room. There was only a cot and a nightstand in the room. A wire window and a thick door faced each other from the walls. I felt dizzy and crashed back to sleep.

When I awoke again, I knew that I was not having a bad dream. They had locked me in a cell. Why had they done that? Where was I? How long would I be there? What was happening to me?

Again I snapped. I started screaming, swearing and crying from the pit of my soul. People dressed in white rushed the door. Someone had a needle. The door opened. I threw the nightstand, then the bed and then my body at the door. It slammed shut. I tore off my gown and began ripping at the skin on my face, neck, chest and back, the skin ravaged by boils, whiteheads and blackheads, the skin I hated with every fiber of my being. I fought them off and mutilated myself until I could no longer hold them back, finally succumbing to the lack of food and sleep.

They said I did not let anyone in the cell for nearly two days. I could not remember. I was too tired and beaten. I had used up everything inside of me. I just wanted to die, right then and there.

The next day, two cops took me from the cell and drove me to a state hospital. Everybody thought that I had gone crazy. The doctors and the judge had decided to commit me to a nut house to see just how crazy I was.

The Harrisburg State Hospital smelled of pee, poop, farts and dying old people. Locked doors and screened windows closed out the real world. Strange old men occupied every nook and cranny of the ward. They did all sorts of odd things: talked to themselves, wet their pants, screamed, beat their heads against walls, laid down and died or sat motionless staring into space. I was scared they would hurt me. I kept my back to the walls and slept with one eye open. My body never stopped twitching.

For 77 scary days and nights, I was tested, questioned and made to feel crazy. A whole summer was shot while the doctors dug through my brain. Their reports used terms like "schizoid," "schizophrenic," "autistic" and "neurotic" to describe my state of mind. A panel of six doctors said that I should stay at the hospital for a long time. They felt I would probably be crazy the rest of my life. Lucky for me, however, my probation officer had them send me home anyway.

Tenth grade began soon after I returned home. Another school accepted me into an Industrial Arts course. I was going to learn about running lathes and other machines, but my mind was not into it. I hated school, life, everything and everybody. I skipped classes and picked fights with anyone that got in my way. My grades were almost all failing.

I turned 16 and quit going to school. Why should I do something that I hated? Why should I let school make me feel like a failure? Maybe I could get a job at a carwash or something.

Mom, the principal and the probation officer did not agree with my reasoning. They said I "needed an education." They would not allow me to quit school, but I refused to go anyway. I was old enough to make up my own mind, I reasoned. Whose life was it anyway?

Back to the detention center I went. The judge did not say much to me. He had already made up his mind. The police were going to drive me to a reform school.

My life seemed hopeless. The pain never ended. It just kept going around and around in a circle. First, I was made to feel unwanted. Then I was made to feel like an ugly failure. Then they said I was crazy. Now I was a criminal. Was pain all there was to life? Was my life doomed to get worse and worse? Would the negativity never end?

The Pennsylvania George Junior Republic was a tough place. Over 350 boys packed the seven cottages where we lived. The courts placed all of us there for breaking laws. The laws we had broken included almost everything but murder. Many of the boys had been in numerous out-of-home placements. Some spent years in detention centers and other reform schools, while still others had endured countless foster-care placements, before their rebellious behaviors landed them at the PJR. We were a sad lot of lost boys.

The first month was the most difficult. New boys had to go through a learning process called "orientation." That is how we learned what the adults expected of us. It was like the Army. Boots and work clothes took the place of street clothing. We marched in columns of twos everywhere. One step out of line and they yelled at, hit or paddled us. There was no room for error. We were bad boys in need of serious discipline.

There were other things to learn, too, like how to survive in the cottage. The boys who had been there longer picked on new arrivals. It was their way of culling out the weak from the strong. The weak boys soon lost their belongings, after the tough boys pushed, beat and used them. Strength brought respect. Weakness promoted pain. "Best wait 'til you've been here a while," was a badge of honor for long-timers, who lorded their seniority over new boys.

The end of orientation meant that I had become a "citizen." The administration placed me in the tenth grade and made sure I attended class. When I was not in school, I had assigned jobs like shining floors, cleaning the church or working on the farm. We were in bed by 10 p.m. and up at 6 a.m. There was little time to get into trouble. Somebody was always watching and waiting for a mistake.

But, reform school did not tolerate mistakes. We were to follow the rules, receiving punishment when we did not. Those caught cheating, lying, stealing, running away, talking back to adults, fighting or breaking other rules paid for their misbehaviors. Punishments included loss of privileges, loss of visits, shaving our heads, hard labor on the farm, shining the floors for hours and punches with a fist or "cracks" with a heavy wooden paddle. The oak paddles were used to "teach us a lesson." My buns took a bruising more than once.

Reform school was not all bad. After a few months, I learned to follow the rules. I also began using my brain. In tenth and eleventh grades, the teachers voted me "outstanding student." I earned almost all As and Bs. I got involved with the school newspaper. My cottage mates voted me captain of several inter-cottage sports teams. The administration selected me to be on the student council. I became a cottage leader. I learned that I could be good at things if I worked hard.

Eighteen months crawled by slowly before release from reform school. The day I put that place behind me marked a new beginning.

There were still many problems to face, though. Troubles at school or home could trip me up. The probation officer watched my every move. Freedom might again be lost with my next mistake. There was something else, too. I was almost 18. I would soon be an adult. That meant that I could go to jail or prison. I did not want to live like that again. I did not want to lose my freedom. I had to take control of my life. My future was in my hands.

That is when I made up my mind to change my life. Nobody else could do it for me. It was up to me to decide what I wanted. It was up to me to make good things happen. It was up to me to stop the circle of pain from going around and around.

Wanting something and making it happen are two different things. I had to have a plan. That meant looking deep inside me, finding my problems and changing them. It did not take long to see that bad behavior was my worst enemy. I had spent most of my life hitting back for the pain I felt: pain for pain. Hurt me, and I hurt you back. Around and around it went in a never-ending circle. There was no winning that game.

Stopping my bad behavior was the way to end the circle of pain. That was difficult. I was used to acting-out my pain. It took me nearly three years to gradually quit striking back at the world, but I knew that if I did not change my bad behavior, I would never straighten out my life.

There were three places I had to change my bad behavior: at home, with other kids and at school. These were the three parts of my life where I always failed. Almost every problem I had came from one of them. I had to find a way to conquer each problem.

Home was at the root of my problems. The years of fighting between Mom and Dad, then the years of fighting between Mom and me, had filled us with pain. We did not know how to be nice to each other or show that we cared. Fighting was all we knew. Mom would tell me to do something, and I would not do it. She would yell at me, and I would yell back at her. Back and forth, around and around it went in yet another never-ending circle.

The best way to change my behavior at home was to listen to Mom, do as she said and not fight with her. That was tough. Some of the things she told me to do seemed dumb, and sometimes I just did not want to do them. Other times I had to bite my tongue to keep from telling her off. It took us time, but we learned to be nice to each other.

Friends were another area of life where I had problems. Most "good" kids treated me like dirt. That is why I became friends with other "bad" kids. We were peers because of the way we led our lives. We all had problems at home or had failed a grade or been in trouble with the law. We were outsiders who had come together to feel less alone. Trouble was all we knew. We did everything together: steal, fight, skip school and act-out our hate and pain.

I no longer wanted to live like that. Hanging out with the old gang meant trouble. That could lead to more problems, including incarceration. I had to meet kids who stayed out of trouble. I needed to make friends with kids who lived the way I wanted to live. One at a time, I made new friends. They introduced me to other kids. Soon I knew many new people. I watched how they acted. I copied their behavior and learned to fit in. People treated me nicely when I was nice to them. I began to feel better about myself.

School was the other place where I had to change my bad behavior. Most of my experiences at school had been bad: flunking subjects, failing a grade, detention, feeling dumb, other students calling me names and treating me like dirt, teachers making a fool of me and the principal throwing me out. I hated school and everything about it.

Little by little, I learned that I had to set goals and meet them. One goal involved making sure I was not locked up again. Another goal was to graduate from high school. I had passed eleventh grade in reform school. I needed to pass only my senior year in public school to graduate. I learned to get along with the students, teachers and principal. Although I graduated 187th in a class of 192 students, my grades were good enough to earn a diploma.

Graduating from high school filled me with strength and pride. I had proven that I was neither dumb nor a failure. I could do anything if I worked hard and made it happen. Nobody could take my diploma away from me. Nobody could make me feel small again. I was going to get stronger and better every day—and I did!

Changing my life was not easy. It took years of hard work to beat the odds and fix my problems. There were times when life got the best of me and I fell backwards. When that happened, I dug deeper and did not quit. There was too much at stake. As the years slipped by, the pain and problems of the past gave way to the promise of the future. Life became what I made of it. I never again got in trouble with the law. I went on to college and earned a doctorate. I worked with or studied delinquent youth at the Pennsylvania Department of Education, the National Center for Juvenile Justice, the Orthogenic School at the University of Chicago and the William Gladden Foundation. I dedicated my life to helping troubled kids, and the professionals who serve them, to understand what is required to transform childhood behavioral and emotional disorders into positive adult outcomes.

Most of my youth, all I knew was rejection, pain, failure and all that is bad and mean in life. There seemed to be no end to it. It was not until I learned to take control of my life and to change it to what I wanted it to be that I finally took charge of my life and my future.

The years I spent in the orphanage, mental health and juvenile justice systems had a profound affect on my adult outcome, both bad and good. For example, had I stayed at the Tressler Lutheran Home until I graduated from high school, the remainder of my adolescence would have been decidedly less tumultuous. Why the administration decided to send me back to the source of my problems still confounds me. To quote their rationale, I was "antisocial" and "not taking advantage of the program." Yes, I did cry and sulk a lot, and I did stay to myself: BIG DEAL! How did they expect an emotionally confused twelve-year-old child to handle separation from his mother and placement with strangers? This was a huge opportunity lost to stop the circle of pain and reclaim my emotional stability. Instead, Lutheran Social Services dropped the ball, and in doing so, condemned me to endure more years of pain, confusion, emotional instability and behavioral problems. Sometimes you get only one chance to reclaim a troubled child, and with each failed attempt, the odds of his or her recovery diminish.

Placement in the Harrisburg State Hospital very easily might have destroyed any chance I had to return to society. How could the Juvenile Court condemn an emotionally immature fifteen-year-old boy to such a horrific place, if it was its purpose to help him? Just being there put my sanity, indeed, my entire future, at risk. I spent two and a half months among crazy adults who might have killed or raped me. I observed, experienced and somehow survived terrifying events and behaviors that still haunt my dreams. That period was the lowest, most agonizing and confusing time in my entire life, from birth until today. Words defy adequate description of the horror, so surreal and absurd was that living nightmare. Were it not for my probation officer's insistence that I be discharged, the six-member panel of psychiatrists who assessed my sanity would have kept me there, perhaps for years, and I would have become what their interviews and tests said I was, "schizoid," "schizophrenic," "autistic," "neurotic." Despite these pejorative diagnoses, however, I have somehow managed a nearly 50-year period of remission, without the aid of mental health counseling or prescription medications.

In sharp contrast to my failed orphanage and mental health interventions, there were heroes in my life, professionals and programs that did promote my turnaround. Chief among these was my probation officer, Mr. Henry Lentz, a no-neck, semi-bald, wrinkly old man whom I hated with a passion while I was under his supervision. As I have matured and put my youth in perspective, including reading the detailed case records he kept on me, however, I now realize just how lucky I was to have such a wise and sincerely dedicated professional working on my behalf. His refusal to accept the negative labels and recommendations of the psychiatrists at the state hospital made all the difference between who I am today and what I may have become. He saved me from ruin, plain and simple.

He did more than just save me from the shrinks, though, he made sure I remained in school and got an education, including committing me to the Pennsylvania George Junior Republic. Taking me out of my dysfunctional family home and placing me in a structured setting during the last half of the tenth grade and the entire eleventh grade proved to be a stroke of genius, although I would have vehemently disagreed with his decision at the time. I matured dramatically during those eighteen months, thanks in large part to two other heroes, William D. Gladden and William H. Gladden, father and son, whose unfettered approach to helping troubled boys become men substituted for the absence of a loving father to serve as a role model. I needed that full eighteen months of structured guidance to change my attitude and gain the maturity to think beyond the moment. Any time less, and the entire change process may not have taken hold. Behaviors do not change instantly, nor do they improve in the milieu that spawned them. Placing me in the appropriate setting for the right amount of time helped me to break the circle of pain and saved me from a lifetime of dysfunction.

An American Odyssey:
Finding One's Way After Foster Care

❦

John Seita

Norman Rockwell had a view of America: idyllic and well-scrubbed, cherub-faced children playing happily under the watchful gaze of protective parents. His artistic perception did not include the likes of me: abandoned, alone, hurting, lost and wondering. There were no happy children playing under the watchful gaze of protective parents in my world.

I was five when I watched my father bash my mother's head against the kitchen wall. Their argument at dinner had been brief. I cannot remember what set him off, but he was like that, ready to fight whenever she said or did something he did not like. He leapt over the garage-sale Formica table and pulled her out of her chair by the hair, a clump of which drifted silently to the floor, then banged her head repeatedly against the kitchen wall, with a crack, crack, crack sound I spent years trying to forget. Streams of dark red blood spurted from her battered skull, splattering the wall.

My mother screamed first, and then she pleaded. I crumpled in the corner and hid my face behind my knees, sobbing, trembling, scared I was next to know his wrath, but yet I could not avert my eyes from his savage assault. The whole time he beat her, I rocked, cried and prayed to die and come back a different boy from a different family where my new father and mother loved each other, like on TV, where everybody is happy, safe and loved. That's all I wanted. What horrible thing had I done to deserve this? Was it my fault? Was I just getting what I deserved? Would my life get better?

"You may as well go ahead and kill me!" my mother screamed toward my father's contorted, vein-swollen red face. Her face looked different, too: a bluish gray that reminded me of a cartoon where the bad guy was beating the good guy, although this was no cartoon.

The beating ended as abruptly as it began. Maybe the blood speckled kitchen wall let him know she was nearly dead. Perhaps her crying awoke him to his brutality or was he simply out of energy?

He dragged my mother to the car. "Are you OK? I didn't mean to hurt you. Are you OK? Please be OK. I won't ever do that again, honey, I promise," he tried to soothe her gently with his voice, as she lay crumpled in a bloody heap in the front seat.

My mother did not reply. She sat slumped near the passenger door sobbing quietly, as if trying to muffle her pain and anguish. I curled up silently in the backseat, pretending I was not there at all. I liked doing that, imagining I was invisible. Over the years, I learned to curl up and hide in plain sight a lot. It was easy to do. They didn't seem to take much notice of me anyway. They were in their own tormented worlds. I was an afterthought.

Sometime after the beating, my father vanished. One day he was there, and the next day he was gone, without so much as a good-bye or see-ya-later. You would think his absence made life better for my mother and me, but even though he beat her, she lamented his loss, leaving her alone to drown her sorrows in an ocean of booze and a stream of men. I was alone too, absent a father and minus a sober mother; I was an orphan in waiting.

My mother was neglectful and abusive. Aside from her poor parenting skills, she also had eight documented incidents of attempted suicide. She suffered violence at the hands of various men throughout her life, leaving her with a sad, tragic reality. Because I was a child, I did not have the maturity to understand her problems. Our home was not a home at all, but a place to endure the helplessness and loneliness of my life.

At the age of eight, the court removed my brother, sister and I from my mother's home and I unwillingly started on an odyssey that would not end until I was well into adulthood.

After the court took us away from our mother, I never saw my sister Maria again. Jimmy and I went to live in the Receiving Home—a huge, old, gray, smelly, ramshackle building in inner city Cleveland, housing kids nobody wanted. The first night away from our equally filthy apartment, I was angry, terrified and unsure of what would happen next. Kneeling beside the rusty, metal-framed bed with the urine-stained mattress, I prayed to ease my pain. My cries for help resounded like wails into an empty universe.

At age nine, I shuttled off to my first foster home placement. My caseworker just swooped me up one day out of the common area in the Receiving Home without warning, put one striped tee shirt, a pair of jeans, two pairs of socks and two pairs of white underwear into a brown paper grocery bag, and spirited me into her county car. I asked quite a few questions about where we were going. She responded by grinning and assuring me that "they are really nice people; you're going to like it there." Then she grinned again, just like the Cheshire cat. She was long on grins, and short on answers. I guess either she didn't know what to say, or perhaps she had nothing to say. Those must have been prerequisite skills for her job. At least her smile was pretty.

My memories of my first foster home are faint and few. I stayed there only a week before I ran away. That was the first of many times I would run from a foster home. It was, after all, a foster home, and I did not belong there. It turned out that I did not belong anywhere. Here is an excerpt from a social work report written on me all those many years ago:

"John's father has openly rejected John in the past and states that he wants nothing to do with him. John is aware of this and is having a tremendous amount of trouble handling this knowledge. Added to this is the knowledge by John of knowing that his

father accepts his brother. John seems not to reject
James because he is living with his father, but seems
quite affectionate toward him and is always anxious and
concerned about how he is doing."

After a few weeks, the court allowed Jimmy to leave the Receiving
Home to live with our father. I still had hopes of returning home, if
not to live with my mother, at least with my father. Imagine my joy
when I was told, "Your dad is here to see you." I sprinted to the lobby
with an ear-to-ear grin, seeking his embrace. We walked lockstep to
his car, where I sat proudly next to my dad on the front seat, awaiting
the good news that he had come to take me home with him. He was
my hero who had come to rescue me from my captors.

My father cranked the rusty old Mercury, which did not
always start on the first try, but to me it was a carriage worthy of
a king. We drove to a nearby drive-in for hamburgers, as fathers
and sons are supposed to do, to share their thoughts and satisfy
their appetites. My back was sore and I sat stiffly. He noticed my
discomfort and complimented me for being a "tough little man" and
not complaining about my pain. I was so proud to please him.

As we drove back to the Receiving Home, he said, "John, I
need to tell you something."

I hoped that he was going to say I was coming home to stay
with him and Jimmy. My smile broadened, my fingers grew tingly,
my heart pounded and I felt as if I were about to float up to Heaven.

"John, you need to know that I am not really your dad. I
don't know who your real dad is, but it's not me," he stumbled to say,
his eyes fixed straight ahead through the cracked windshield.

The world crashed around me. What did he say? Was he just
goofing on me? I refused to believe him. If he was not my father,
who was? Then my heart began screaming inside my shaking body.
I sat stiff and straight, and when the tears started, I turned away, as
if I were looking out the window. Not a word passed my lips. When
we pulled up to the curb by the Receiving Home, I glanced out the
corner of my eye toward him. Our eyes never met. I strained to push

open the heavy car door with my shoulder and stepped out onto the crumbling concrete, walking slowly up the stairs to the building, giving him time to call me back and say he changed his mind. The only sound I heard was that of the Mercury's tires squealing away and my broken heart pounding in my chest. My head hung low; I came to realize that he was gone . . . forever.

Following that fateful day, I moved roughly fifteen times over the next eleven years. Each new placement drove another nail into my broken heart. Nobody wanted me. I was nothing more than worthless human garbage shifted from one foster home to another, the son of an unknown father and an alcoholic mother, neither of whom gave a damn about me, and the ward of a system that did not know what to do with me. With each new placement, I drew further into myself, cutting off my emotions and separating myself from the rest of the world. If nobody wanted me, then I wanted nobody. To Hell with everybody, it's just me against them!

Although I somehow survived this long string of placements in foster homes, group homes and various institutions such as orphanages and detention homes, my emotions and behaviors changed radically. I often stole food and other items, ran away repeatedly and engaged in numerous petty crimes. I was at war with the world.

In 1967, at the age of twelve, the court placed me at the Starr Commonwealth, a residential boys' home where I lived for the next seven years. Even after "graduating" from Starr as a nineteen-year-old, the odyssey continued. Starr and its staff abandoned me to the streets, leaving me to fend for myself, an angry, lonely, largely antisocial and ill-prepared adolescent with no family and no support services to help me make the difficult transition into a society that now expected me to function as a responsible adult. Imagine being a ship without a rudder, drifting aimlessly as you struggle to learn how to steer yourself in the right direction without the benefit of map or compass. That's how I learned to navigate in society and, unfortunately, what tens-of-thousands of other kids exiting placement each year must learn on their own. No wonder so many of us fail. I am one of the lucky ones.

At best, my transition to independence was treacherous. Easing into adulthood and its responsibilities is difficult for many young adults, but my situation was especially so because I lost my most important connections. Without a family, I expected no phone calls from home, because there was no home. There were no requests for "care packages," for who would prepare and send them? There was no one to ask for money, and there was no one to help me navigate the confusing and Byzantine world of college. I had no one to cheer me on or, if necessary, to kick me in the rear as I faced the challenges of college.

Most high school graduates go away to college with a sense of excitement and a yearning for independence. Of course, while they make plans to enjoy the freedom that college life will afford them, they completely take for granted the security system backing them up. They have parents, a home, and access to money and, if everything fails, a warm place to return to and lick their wounds before trying again to tackle the world on their own.

As I embarked on this same new adventure, however, I did so with a great sense of fear and no support system at all. I once again felt abandoned in almost all ways. I was adjusting to something new on my own, as I had so many times before. I did not know what to expect and was not successful in making friends to help me through the transition to adulthood.

The child welfare system did a poor job on my behalf upon emancipation. With only a couple of exceptions, those adults whom I had relied on over the past few years were now inaccessible. Legally and physically, I was an adult, with the entire attendant opportunities to achieve. Socially and emotionally, though, I was very immature. I was aware of this even while experiencing it, but I felt I had nowhere to turn for counsel.

I was just as alone as I had been as an eight-year-old boy in Cleveland. I would go for long drives and allow myself to wonder: Why should I live? Perhaps I could crash my car into a tree or do something equally dramatic to rid myself of the burdens of living. The truth was my expectations for college life had been sorely disappointed. I hated being at college and I hated feeling so lost and alone.

At least when I was an eight-year-old in the child welfare system there was some required pretense on the part of others to care about me and keep track of my whereabouts. The scope of my personal responsibility when I was a child was limited, as was my ability to handle things on my own. No one expected much of me, but now that I was nineteen, I had to assume one hundred percent of the responsibility for my own behaviors. Despite this fact, I received very little in the way of preparation for what I was experiencing or for what was to come.

While my level of maturity made this dramatic shift in my life less painful than when I was eight, I was only slightly less scared. The consequences I would face this time would be much more treacherous and unpredictable. I felt like a failure for my limited ability to cope in this brave new world. I did try to reach out for help, but felt only limited success in doing so. The people around me seemed to keep saying, "You can do it," but no one told me how. Their advice lacked utility and common sense. I had entered a life that compromised me spiritually, socially and economically. I felt doomed and destined to fail.

Upon release from Starr, the time had come for me to join the ranks of society. More than a transition from institutionalized child to emancipated adult, it would be a transformation, forever changing my status in life, marking the end of my foster care journey and signaling a new beginning. It was not a transforming event, however. Instead, my transition marked a continuation of old patterns in new settings.

I left foster care unprepared for reintegration to society, with few resources to cope with a sometimes harsh and unsympathetic world. I had no family, few contacts and a general distrust of people that further hindered success. Conversely, my assets included many of the values I embraced at Starr and a few contacts that offered temporary but insufficient support.

I accept responsibility for my actions as a young adult, yet my personal history, the context of my life and my poor preparation for independent living clearly influenced the choices I made. After all, one makes choices within the context of the life one is living and the tools one has. I had a piss-poor context and a major lack of social and practical tools.

Leaving foster care is not to be confused with putting the impact of foster care behind. There are aftershocks following years of institutional care, and I clearly bore the brunt of them. Many young adults will experience these unsettling and sometimes-devastating tremors until the system understands how to prepare foster care alumni to integrate successfully back into society.

It can take years of successful independence for those of us who grow up as troubled kids to leave our past behind. My research with foster care alumni reveals that even those who are successful by most standards still bear the repercussions of foster care. They often have faint, but visible scars. Some harbor hatred and bitterness, and the littered dreams of a lost family. I do not believe that leading scarred lives is inevitable. Like others with disabilities, it is possible to become stronger by having survived trauma. Sometimes the experience of great loss or defeat helps us reflect on the real meaning of our existence.

There are neither easy answers nor a blueprint for how one might reclaim one's life out of tragedy. For me the journey has been satisfying, but draining, full of doubt and fear, and, at times, frustration and anger. Therefore, I guard against too much satisfaction. I sometimes still expect the worst outcome and remain suspicious when life seems to be going too well. Deep down inside, I dread that when good things happen to me, something bad is bound to follow. This negative outlook has haunted me since childhood, although less and less over time, but it has never been fully extinguished.

From my conversations with other former foster children, I know I am not alone in harboring negative feelings of uncertainty. The underlying belief that we are somehow unworthy of happiness and success weighs heavy on too many of us. It restrains us from enjoying the sweet spots of life seemingly so easily embraced by those who had the good fortune to reap the rewards of secure childhoods provided by loving and supportive parents. Living with strangers in out-of-home placement further accentuates the belief that we are unworthy—indeed, worthless—because we have no connection to the most basic of all human institutions—the biological family. Instead, we often experienced loveless, even abusive, placements in foster homes and institutions. Perhaps this is a reason why so many of us fail at mastering the difficult transition from foster child to emancipated adult. Kicked to the streets, we must learn to survive without the safety net of family to pick us up when we fall and provide supportive guidance until we regain our balance. I was fortunate not to go the way of so many of my brother and sister foster children who succumb to adjustment problems such as poverty, homelessness, pregnancy, prostitution, imprisonment, substance abuse and premature death. It is this feeling that I am one of the lucky ones that spurs me on to clear a path for the foster kids who may not share my good fortune.

More and more, I am of the opinion that part, if not much of the problem with the child welfare system, is that most of those administering and leading the system have never experienced it as a consumer of its services and seldom do they seek guidance and input from their clients. This is a bit like asking a third-generation millionaire to explain poverty and develop methods to eradicate homelessness. Who is better equipped to know the nuances required to safeguard and reclaim troubled and disenfranchised youth, current and former troubled and disenfranchised youth or persons of privilege who have studied or worked with them? One cannot know something entirely if one has not experienced it. Perhaps that is one of the reasons America's foster care system continues to fail the needs of its vulnerable clients.

"You're an orphan, right? Do you think I'd know
the first thing about how hard your life has been, how
you feel, who you are because I read Oliver Twist? Does
that encapsulate you?"

The above quote from the movie *Good Will Hunting* was part of a
conversation between a therapist and a bitter foster care alumnus,
Will Hunting, played by Matt Damon. This exchange captures
the difference between living the experience of being an orphan
or merely studying it. Yet, findings contained within a recent
study of private Michigan child welfare agencies conducted by
the School of Social Work at Michigan State University and the
Michigan Federation of Children and Families, show none of
the sample of responding agencies have any foster care alumni
in leadership roles within their agencies. Based upon anecdotal
evidence, there is no reason to suspect results nationwide differ
from those in Michigan. The lack of personal experience of child
welfare executives and leaders might be a serious handicap in
understanding and implementing the subtle nuances required for
systemic improvement.

Making the case for building the capacity of foster care
alumni to assume leadership roles in child welfare agencies is the
obvious fact that Caucasians do not dictate policy for the NAACP
or the Urban League. Men do not determine the mission of the
National Organization of Women; heterosexuals do not fight for the
rights of the Gay and Lesbian Alliance, and 20-something whiz-kids
do not lead the American Association of Retired Persons. Doesn't it
make obvious sense that foster care alumni do likewise?

Peter's Story

PHIL QUINN

Sometimes in our efforts to help someone, we hurt that person. For example, the infliction of one type of pain to relieve another type of pain is common in medical treatment. Nonetheless, medical professionals attempt to measure the pain they inflict in their effort to heal against the pain they seek to relieve to insure that their intervention is truly therapeutic and in the best interest of the patient's health. It is the intention that the pain inflicted by administering a shot of antibiotics, for instance, will relieve the discomfort and suffering of infection. Similarly, just as some pain is unavoidable in many medical procedures, some degree of trauma is inevitable whenever social work professionals intervene in a child's life in an effort to relieve his or her suffering.

Too often, intentionality is the primary focus of our intervention evaluation. We assume that the good intentions of caring foster parents, for example, will necessarily result in good effects for the adjudicated child placed in their care and custody. In too many cases, however, this is a potentially faulty and dangerous assumption.

There is a measure of ignorance in all knowledge. Knowledge is a constantly unfolding revelation in which we will know more tomorrow than we do today. Even well-intentioned parents and caregivers can do great harm to a developing child—not out of intent or maliciousness, but out of ignorance. Who among the older generation doubted the wisdom inherent in the aphorism, "sticks and stones can break my bones but words can never harm me," when contemporary knowledge clearly warns that, "sticks and stones can break my bones and words can break my heart"? It is imperative for the well-being of the child that the effects of our intervention undergo constant study and evaluation to assure that our good intentions eliminate bad outcomes. Few decisions are more harmful to children than to remove them from an environment of threat or deprivation and place them in another environment even more deprived or threatening.

Consider the pain inflicted upon five-year-old Peter in a well-intentioned effort by interveners to bring him relief.

• • •

With his Stetson pushed far back on his head, the tall deputy sheriff knelt awkwardly on the uncarpeted wooden floor. Wiping the sweat from his face with the bandanna around his neck, he bent as far forward as possible, straining to see the boy through the gloom under the bed. The contrasting glare of the late afternoon August sunlight that filled the room through the bare windows hurt his eyes as they struggled to adjust to the darkness, but he could see the small boy huddled in the far corner under the bed, just beyond his reach.

"Now Peter, you come on out of there!" the deputy's weary voice commanded. Seeing no movement under the bed, the man sighed deeply and tried once more. "Son, listen to me. I am not here to hurt you. I want to help you and your mother. There is no need to be afraid. Why don't you be a good boy and come on out now? Come on now. Here, I'll give you a hand," he pleaded as he reached as far as he could under the bed.

Five-year-old Peter lay coiled in the furthest corner away from the man, his legs drawn up tightly under his chin, ready to lash out if the hand should come too close. With his back pressed firmly against the base of the wall behind him, his hands clung tenaciously to the rusty bedsprings just above his head. Setting his jaw in fierce determination, the boy tensed the muscles in his arms and legs and waited.

The hand reached slowly for one of the boy's feet. Within inches of its target, the foot shot out with the force of frightened, young muscled legs, smashing the outstretched hand hard into the ragged bedsprings. The deputy yelped painfully as the bedsprings gouged pieces of flesh from the top of his hand.

The standoff ended a short time later as the deputy followed the suggestion of the boy's mother and offered to buy him a chocolate milkshake. It always made Peter feel special when his father would buy him a chocolate milkshake, on those few occasions when he came to see him.

Peter allowed the deputy to pull him from under the bed and place him in the back seat of the squad car. It was not until the car pulled away from the curb that he began to realize what was happening to him. Like a frenzied, caged animal, he was suddenly on his hands and knees in the back seat searching out his mother and two younger brothers still on the front porch of the house.

He clawed at the door frantically trying to get out. When the door would not budge, he scrambled madly across the vinyl seat to the other door, jerking wildly at the handle. Just as he started over the front seat, a large hand closed around his neck and forced him onto his back on the rear seat. With his arms and legs flailing, he fought to free himself from the grip of the giant hand imprisoning his neck. Gnashing his teeth at the arm in front of him, all fight left Peter suddenly, as the sting of a palm slapped against his cheek plunged him into silent surrender.

Hating himself bitterly for betraying his mother and brothers, Peter rested his head in dismay on the window glass behind him. As the car began winding its way into another world far from the one he had known, Peter watched as his mother's head suddenly dropped into her lap, her gaunt body wracked with sobs. Although he had no idea why the deputy had taken him from his mother, he somehow sensed that he would never live with her again. The silent scream that began in his heart and overflowed his mind found no outlet through his mouth, but continued long after his mother was lost from sight. He would be well into adulthood before he could eat a chocolate milkshake again without getting sick.

. . .

This was Peter's first exposure to that round seal on the side of a state car and the people who work behind that seal seeking to bring help and protection to those unable to help or protect themselves. It would not be his last.

Peter's father was Native American. His mother was British. They met in a convalescent hospital on the outskirts of London near the end of World War II. In 1946, they married, returned to the United States and settled near the reservation so that they could be near his paternal family. There were five children in five years—four boys and a girl. Peter was the middle child.

As Peter neared his fifth birthday, his parents divorced. The court awarded custody of his older brother and sister to his father. His mother retained custody of his two younger brothers and himself. Challenged by undiagnosed and untreated symptoms of post-traumatic stress disorder arising from her years in war ravaged London, migration from a British to an American culture, an interracial marriage and then the loss of almost all financial and family support through the divorce, she kept the kids fed, housed and clothed by utilizing welfare and government food commodities. In an attempt to help herself and her boys, she remarried; this time to a man she did not love. Her hope was that he would grow to love—or perhaps tolerate—the three boys enough to reunite the family. This hope died when she became pregnant with his first child.

Peter and his two younger brothers spent the next two years living separately in numerous foster homes, always returning to their mother after a few months on trial reunification visits. They were never successful. Foster placement became more permanent when Peter, at the age of seven, returned home from school one day to watch two men carry his mother out of the house on an ambulance stretcher. For the next several years, Peter and his brothers lived in foster care, sometimes together, sometimes apart, until the Quinn family adopted all three of them on December 7, 1960.

• • •

Placing a child in a foster or adoptive home is similar to grafting an organ to the body. One of two things will typically occur: the body will accept the grafted organ and it will thrive, or the body will reject the organ and it will die. If the body rejects the grafted organ, immediate removal is required or else a traumatic—or perhaps lethal—pathology may develop. Knowing whether the body will accept or reject the graft requires a long period of post-surgical assessments and evaluations. A similar period of supervisory assessments and evaluations is critical to assure the successful and therapeutic placement of a child in a foster or adoptive family.

While there is much to be said for providing children basic life sustaining necessities, such as food, shelter and clothing, it is clear that, by themselves, they do not provide enough substance for a child to thrive. Children must be rooted in an environment rich in emotional acceptance and support, an atmosphere teeming with mental and physical stimulation, one in which they are challenged by endless wonders and possibilities. One of the greatest tragedies of our modern times involves the tens-of-thousands of American youth who are silently and with little notice psychologically, emotionally and spiritually hemorrhaging to death. Once again, consider the case of Peter whose adoption provided him basic life necessities but placed him in a toxic environment that nearly destroyed him.

• • •

Buried desperately under the blankets on the bed, ten-year-old Peter curled into a tight knot as he tried to escape the growing terror evolving around him. He could hear their muffled voices coming from the living room through the bedroom door. Not wanting to hear the harsh words, he strained to concentrate on the sound of their voices. He was safe as long as he could hear the voices, but once the voices stopped, his parents would go to bed and he would be safe until morning—or they would come for him.

Suddenly the voices from the living room became agonizingly quiet. Probing the threatening silence with his every sense, the small boy's heart pounded fiercely against his aching chest. His throat constricted so that he could barely breathe, as he recognized the dreaded sound of feet shuffling across carpet in his direction.

Like an explosion in the darkness, the bedroom door crashed open. Clutching the blankets over his head, Peter pressed hard against the mattress, praying that it would absorb him, encapsulate and protect him from what he knew was to come. The boy began urinating uncontrollably under the blankets as his body shook violently with fear. In a flash, the blankets that had protected him ripped forcefully from his grasp. A rough, hard hand wrapped itself around his ear and pulled him head first out of bed and onto the floor.

"Stand up!" his adoptive father's voice demanded as the hand around his ear painfully pulled him out of the bedroom into the lighted living room where his adoptive mother awaited with glowering eyes. Peter began crying uncontrollably as he spied the row of switches and rubber hose lying on the floor beside her chair. The soggy pajama bottoms drooped in a heap around his ankles, leaving him standing naked in the middle of the living room to face his adoptive parents.

His father's hand slapped hard against the side of his head as the boy bent slowly to pull up his pajamas, sending him sprawling across the floor. His mother mocked him for wetting his clothes as he struggled to regain his feet, threatening to diaper him.

For long moments, his parents stared threateningly at him, as he stood naked and shivering in front of them. Then upon him came their cruel judgment.

"It's time that you learned once and for all who is boss in this family," his father declared.

"When we tell you to do something, we expect you to do it without question, complaint or hesitation," his mother said. "Do you understand?"

"Yes, ma'am," Peter screeched through his parched throat.

"Look at me when you talk to me!" demanded his mother.

Peter cringed inside, as his eyes met her hard, merciless stare.

"I don't think he does understand," accused his father. "I think he needs a lesson to convince him."

Peter began to cry uncontrollably. He knew his lesson would include a beating.

Determined that Peter should learn the importance of being obedient and submissive to them, his parents made the frightened boy stand on his tiptoes, his hands extended as far as they could reach above his head. It was hard for him to keep his balance standing in that position. He reached for the sky, nonetheless, straining every muscle and ligament in his little body to remain straight and unwavering. The next part of his "obedience training" required even more discipline. He had to take one blow from a switch or hose across the stomach and groin area of his body without showing any physical or emotional reaction. Otherwise, the blows would continue until he obeyed.

The lesson ended when Peter collapsed unconscious on the living room floor. By then, his arms and legs were badly cut, scratched and bruised. His parents placed his still naked and bleeding body back into the bed. The next morning the blood had dried and the sheets stuck to his wounds. His parents had to soak him in a bathtub of warm water to free the sheets from his bloody body. His stomach was so swollen and distended that he literally had to carry it in his little hands for the next few days.

. . .

Being the oldest, and so the "ring leader" of what his parents believed was a child conspiracy against them and all authority, Peter became the target of most of their wrath and abuse. They repeatedly physically, emotionally and sexually abused him over the next six years.

By age twelve, Peter had made crucial decisions that would shape the course of his life into adulthood. First was that he did not want to hurt anymore. The best way not to hurt, he concluded, was not to feel. If you do not feel, you cannot hurt. Much of his adolescence, Peter focused on finding ways to avoid, deny, escape or sedate feelings. Equally important was his conclusion that relationships are transient, not something to build upon, but something to use and exploit and then release. Most damaging of all was the dawning awareness that something must be fundamentally wrong with him. Why else would people who said that they loved him want to hurt and reject him? Why else would all those foster families not want him? Why else would his own parents not want him?

His adoptive parents physically and emotionally dominated Peter during his early adolescence. That domination began to erode when Peter noticed they now had to look up at him, as he had grown to over six feet in height. He also realized that he had a world in books that he could retreat to where their caustic words could not touch him, when the pain of their blows no longer sent him to the edge of madness as before.

Their domination ended forever the night Peter decided that he now had the power to hit as hard as them, to run as fast as them, to shout as loud as them, to inflict the kind of pain on them that they had inflicted on him all those years. He decided that the only way to free his brothers and himself from their control was to kill them before they killed him. The planning began.

His parents sensed a change in Peter, and, apparently, it frightened them. They threw him out the front door with the command, "Don't you ever set foot in this house again." He began his life on the street with thirty-seven cents and the clothes on his back. His brothers soon followed. Actually, his parents probably saved his life by throwing him out on the street, Peter concluded years later. If he had stayed in their home, he would have tried to kill his parents. He does not know if he would have succeeded—but he would have tried. If he had tried and been successful killing his parents, he would be in prison or dead today. He owed them at least that much.

Unable to join a military in desperate need of "warm bodies" to send to Viet Nam, due to tunnel vision in his left eye from retinal hemorrhaging caused by his adoptive parents' blows to his head, he had to survive on the street. Having no transportation, no home address (he lived under a pier on the beach), no work clothes, no social security number—all the things needed to have a job, Peter was turned down job after job.

Depressed, angry and desperately hungry, Peter was digging scraps of food from garbage cans along the beach one day when some bikers stopped near him. They watched him for a few minutes, and then they invited him to sit behind one of the riders on his motorcycle. The bikers gave him something to eat, a place to stay, an identity and most especially a "family group" that he could count on for support and protection. Many of them had come from backgrounds similar to his.

Suddenly freed of the mental, physical and emotional domination of his adoptive parents, and now safely accepted and supported in a world of society's throwaways, all the years of abuse, betrayal, anger, repressed rage and pain began to surface in Peter with violent effect. He became a renegade, an outlaw, calculating and mean.

For all the qualities he lacked, Peter believed that his one redeeming asset was his intellect. Although life with the bikers was satisfying in many ways, it did nothing to challenge his intellect, while, at the same time, reminding him hauntingly of his adoptive parent's conclusion that he did not deserve the air he breathed.

One of the bikers taught Peter to play chess. Peter fixated on the game until he mastered it. The skills he learned of planning, strategy, move and counter move, attack and retreat, sacrifice and gain, he began applying to his own life that seemed so unmanageable and out of control. He soon discovered that he could make little changes that would make his life more satisfying. Soon, though, that was not good enough. He did not just want to survive—he had done that! Nor did he just want to live—he was doing that too! Now, he wanted to thrive and pursue a life he so envied of others with careers, families and friendships.

To embrace a positive future, we must turn loose of a negative past, Peter decided. He moved to another city, sold his Harley and entered junior college. It took him four years to complete those first two years of college, but he did it! After earning a bachelor's and master's degree, he worked his way through a doctoral program at Vanderbilt University.

After finishing graduate school, Peter launched a career as a national educator in the field of child abuse prevention and treatment. He keynoted hundreds of national, regional and state conferences throughout the United States and appeared on numerous radio and television talk shows. To date he has authored six books and several articles.

The most damaging and untreated emotional effects of Peter's early life occurred in three major areas.

1. *Betrayal of intrinsic, basic trust.* Children know instinctively that their survival depends on the good will and best intentions of their parents and caregivers. They must literally trust them with their lives. Quick and appropriate response to an infant's crying from hunger, for example, supports intrinsic trust that parents and caretakers can be trusted to relieve discomfort and supply life necessities. Reinforced continually over a period of early childhood, this intrinsic trust becomes the emotional basis for all future successful relationships. Conversely, one must ask this obvious question: What happens

to the children who learn through abuse or neglect that they cannot trust their parents or caregivers to take care of them, who learn they cannot even trust their parents or caregivers to love them without hurting them? Rather than learning to trust his parents and caregivers with his welfare, Peter learned that his natural attachment and dependence upon his biological and adoptive parents made him vulnerable and that vulnerability was dangerous and frightening. Survival demanded detachment and a sense of invulnerability that comes through self-reliance and independence. Children who must "fend for themselves" in an environment of neglect or abuse are likely to adopt immature methods to achieve maturation goals. The result is often adaptive behaviors, perhaps appropriate for survival but maladaptive for learning and socialization. Peter learned to distrust other people's intentions—and even their ability to give him what he wanted or needed. As a result, distrust became the emotional basis of his future relationships.

The loss of intrinsic trust in his parent(s) and caregivers to truly love and accept him, as well as truly care about his wellbeing, did not just hurt Peter as a child growing up—it impaired him. It impaired his ability to bond, to attach himself at a deep psychological and emotional level to another human being; it impaired his ability to establish and sustain long-term intimate human relationships. It impaired his ability to entrust his life and wellbeing to the care of another. A life of few friendships, a tendency toward social isolation and failed marriages has been the long-term consequence.

2. *A deeply rooted sense of personal shame.* Guilt can be an appropriate human response when it motivates us to assume responsibility for the things we say and do, or do not say and do, correct our behavior, make amends and not repeat the same mistakes again. Shame, however, is never an appropriate response for a child. We tend to feel guilty about our acts of omission or commission that embarrass, hurt or deprive others, but we do

not feel as much ashamed of our acts as we do of ourselves. We feel ashamed of who and what we are as males or females, sons or daughters, husbands or wives. We feel ashamed of our selves—our very beings. Children learn early on that they can control their words and deeds to earn parental or caregiver acceptance and approval. They also learn there is nothing they can change about themselves to earn the love of their parents or caregivers. They are who they are but can behave in ways pleasing or displeasing to others. When parents or caregivers focus punitive attention upon what children have no control to change, they may provoke deep feelings of personal inadequacy and shame. Shaming children breeds helplessness into their developing psychology. Once we breed helplessness into a child's psychology, we have planted the seeds of the addictive personality. One way to understand addiction is as a desperate attempt to overcome feelings of shame and helplessness when we feel bad. Shaming Peter did not just hurt him—it impaired him. It impaired his ability to grow into a non-addictive personality.

3. *Double binds and existential paradoxes.* Again, children know instinctively that they must remain in close emotional and physical contact with their parents and caregivers in order to survive. Survival demands physical and emotional intimacy. Again, however, we must ask the question: What happens to the child who learns that physical and emotional intimacy with parents and caregivers too often results in physical, emotional or sexual violence that threatens their survival? A psychological double bind occurs when survival requires intimacy and yet intimacy threatens survival. These are contradictory demands of survival. This is an existential paradox. How is a child to meet the contradictory demands of survival when it involves loving and hating, trusting and distrusting, being physically and emotionally intimate and avoiding physical and emotional intimacy, being attached and detached, being attracted and repelled to and by the same person—because survival demands it? The natural

response of most human personalities is to develop emotional, physical and behavioral symptoms in order to cope with the high levels of stress, fear and anxiety created by such intense, paradoxical internal conflicts. Much of Peter's problematic psychological, emotional and behavioral symptoms in childhood and adolescence were rooted in his immature and adaptive efforts to resolve the contradictory demands of survival imposed upon him by neglectful and abusive parents and caregivers. The many double binds imposed upon Peter did not just hurt him; they may very well have impaired his mental and emotional health.

Most of Peter's recovery involved actively grieving for a lost and damaged childhood. He replaced his lost family with the bikers. He replaced the loss of his innocent self with a tarnished image. He replaced his helplessness with acts of brutality. He grieved the loss of stability in his life by threatening the stability in others' lives. He expressed his pain through acts of rage.

Recovery for Peter involved finding appropriate ways of expressing his grief through meaningful activity. He replaced the bikers with a wife and children. He reclaimed a part of his lost self by earning a doctorate degree. He replaced his tarnished image by becoming a committed Christian. He learned to avoid the rejection and reprisals of others by doing praiseworthy things and becoming an overachiever. He replaced violent acts used to express his rage with even more powerful tools of expression: written and spoken words!

For years, Peter has written and spoken his anger and pain to audiences all over this country and others. In sharing his pain, he addresses the suffering of all victims of abuse. He became a child advocate and dedicated his life to protecting children from abuse. Every time Peter writes or speaks out, he is expressing and resolving his own grief, mourning not only the loss of his own childhood, but grieving over the loss of innocence he knows with certainty occurred in countless homes to countless lives all across this country last night, the night before that and the night before that one.

Recovery for Peter involved turning loose of what is lost—of what is hurting him—and taking hold of the opportunity for new life and new beginnings each day brings; but before turning loose, he documented his losses in his memoir *Cry Out!*, his written testimonial to the will and power of a child's spirit to prevail against overwhelming odds.

Recovery for Peter involved a series of actions involving release and embrace: Tempus Praeteritum Resolve ET Carpe Diem—release the past and seize the day!

. . .

Children deserve our best efforts. Their future and ours demands it. While many professionals who work with or on behalf of children in care do stellar jobs of serving and protecting them, it is imperative that they avoid complacency and apathy by constantly challenging themselves with new knowledge, deeper insights and strategies that are more effective. I think we must seek systemic change in several important areas.

1. Recognize and understand that childhood is not what we do while we are waiting to grow up, an immature condition that must be outgrown. It is not just a critical stage in the development of a healthy adult personality; it is equally a wonderful state of human existence with its own integrity, joys and challenges.

2. Constantly monitor with the intent to minimize the trauma of intervention and its consequences in the lives of children. Research and education are important aids in our quest to make helping more therapeutic and less traumatic.

3. Adopt a lengthy period of supervisory assessment and evaluation of all placements in residential, foster or adoptive environments. We must not assume that any placement is a good placement for every child. Just as some adults live and function best in certain environments, children live and function better in certain environments than they do in others.

4. Avoid punishing children for being normal. Anger, for example, is the second recognized stage of grief. This natural stage of the grieving process is too often misunderstood and too often punished, forcing children to suppress, deny, delay or avoid this most important step in the healing process. Unacknowledged and unexpressed pain can have serious developmental and behavioral consequences.

5. Pursue permanency in every placement. Children must develop healthy root systems to thrive. Root systems do not develop in transient lifestyles. Root systems encourage attachment and involvement in the family, school and community.

There is hope for Peter and others like him because there are caring, committed people who have dedicated their lives and careers to the welfare of children; people who, despite the low pay, criticism, lack of appreciation and constant frustration, have dedicated themselves to improving the services and outcomes of children such as Peter. Because all those faceless people, whose names he will never know, who interfaced with him at various times in his life, did not quit on him and go do something less stressful and more profitable, he is here today. I can say that with certainty because I am Peter.

Coming Full Circle:
From Child Victim to Childcare Professional

⁂

ANGELIQUE DAY

Like so many American kids reared by abusive and neglectful parents, I did not know the simple joys of childhood, nor was I permitted the normalcy of a stable family life. By my ninth birthday, I had heard about the "Great American Dream," and although I wanted to believe in it—desperately—it was nothing more than a little girl's wistful fantasy. In my world, nightmares dominated dreams, and fantasies existed only briefly, extinguished by the daily horrors of cruel reality. What did manage to persist unabated was physical and mental abuse given freely and in abundance by a mother who should have loved and protected us.

The initial report of my mother's abusiveness occurred in 1978. It happened while she was pregnant with me. The object of her abuse was my four-year-old brother. Two weeks later, the authorities filed a second report of abuse and neglect. When the child welfare system tried to help my mother, my father moved us out of state. I was born in 1979 in North Carolina, the second child of six. Another sister followed just ten months later.

In 1981, we returned to our home state. Over the next few years, we grew to a family of five children. We lived in a small town a long way from relatives. My mother had no siblings, and my father avoided nearly all interaction with his family. He accepted a job that often took him out of state. When he was not on the road, he spent his "family time" at the local bar, which resulted in increased fighting and screaming between my parents. His addiction to alcohol and absence from our home quickly became a customary pattern. During these frequent times of absence, my mother grew increasingly lonely and bitter. Deep depression set in. She refused to discuss her feelings with my father, but her anger exploded the moment he was gone. She cursed us and accused us of being at fault for her problems. Many times, so many times, I cannot count them, I prayed silently in my thoughts: Please God! Please make her stop! Please don't let her hit us anymore! Please protect us! Please make her love us! Please stop the pain! I'll do better! I'll be a good daughter! I promise! Please! Please! Please!

My older brother and I became her punching bags. Her temper was short, quick and too often without reason. The beatings continued on a daily basis. My mother was a large woman and her fists felt like steel hammers battering our small frail bodies. Often, she grabbed anything in sight with which she could beat us: a hairbrush, my dad's belt, large metal serving spoons, pots and pans, mops, brooms, a wooden cutting board, you name it, she used it to "teach us a lesson."

Finally, after years of being the recipients of her anger and frustration, my brother and I decided we could not take it anymore. We ran away into the woods near our home. Twenty-four hours later, the police found us, and took us to the police station, where a Child Protective Services worker interrogated us in front of our mother. We both knew better than to tell the truth about why we left. My mother's warning stare let us know without speaking a word that we would receive the beating of our life, so we lied. We blamed it on school. My mother smiled. That was the last day she allowed us outside to play.

You would think someone had to see our bruised and battered bodies, but my mother was too clever to leave visible marks. She hit us in places where our clothing covered the cuts, bruises and scabs. She was so good at her abuse—and so proud of her ability to get away with it—that she instructed us in detail how to beat our own children and get away with it. At her most horrible mental breakdown, she asked my brother to kill our father. Fortunately, he was too scared to follow through with this request.

In due course, a sixth child was born, three months premature, weak and sickly. He remained in the hospital fighting for his life for three months. Upon his release, the doctor ordered the services of a community health nurse to monitor his progress. That is when mother stopped cooking and cleaning the house, and ordered the three oldest children to do it: my brother, sister and me. We were also responsible for all the grocery shopping. We fought over this chore because we could ride our bikes to the store. Our bikes were a main source of transportation, as my mother did not have a driver's license and did not own a car.

My parents failed to take proper care of the baby. They refused to take him for his medical checkups. This resulted in another Child Protective Services report of abuse and neglect. When the community health nurse came to check up on the baby, the filthy house and the way we were living sickened her. She also found the baby with a bloody and scarred bottom and open wounds from lying too long in his own feces.

Child Protective Services opened a case on our family and we received case management for six months. According to the case records, the pediatrician warned the caseworker that my mother was mentally "losing it."

The Child Protective Services worker alerted the school about our family situation. We were to see the school counselor, and he was to alert the Child Protective Services worker if he noticed anything suspicious. The school counselor was a tall hard-looking man who made me feel very uncomfortable answering his questions. Maybe if he knew more about the physical and emotional signs of abuse, he would have known what questions to ask me, or perhaps if he had the sensitivity of a woman, I would have found the courage to reveal everything, but I did not. I could not risk the consequences of exposing our "family secret," so I kept my mouth sealed tight about the terrible things our mother did to my brother and me. Fear of reprisal makes martyrs of frightened children.

The records indicate the school counselor never contacted the Child Protective Services worker, so it was "assumed" that everything at home was fine. Child Protective Services closed the case with no additional follow up, leaving my brother and me to suffer the continued assaults of our mother. Why could nobody see what was happening to us?

My mother got worse psychologically, and she began having serious physical problems. As we children grew older, the beatings became harder and more frequent. Maybe we did something wrong, or maybe it was just the look on our faces that set her off into fits of uncontrollable rage. There was no knowing what to expect from her; she seemed to lose it without the slightest sign of provocation, which kept us on a heightened sense of emotional arousal and fear.

There was an occasion when my mother, in a psychotic state, was convinced that the devil had entered my brother's body. In a "heroic" attempt, she tried to beat the devil out of him. She hit him hard in the face; blood poured from his nose. She ripped the hair from his head in clumps; I watched helplessly as she threw the hair to the floor. She straddled my brother's chest, jumping up and down to the point where he could not breathe. I had to assault her to stop her cruelty. I thought she was going to kill him. Even at my young age, I knew we were in trouble and that something was terribly wrong with her. We were all terrified, the six of us so frightened and confused that at times we huddled tightly together in a corner, crying and begging her to stop. Still, nobody came to rescue us and we remained in that horrible house of pain.

My brother and I tried to tell my father on his rare visits home about the beatings. He turned us a deaf ear. He did not want to hear the truth. I realize now, he already knew about the abuse and neglect, and that he did not care. His own life was all that mattered to him, and our mother's love for him became her single all-consuming obsession. We kids were lost somewhere in the recesses of their self-absorption. She told us repeatedly, "It's your father—not me - who wanted you." I believe she resented our being born because she thought we stole his affections from her. Of course, that was not true, but I think she blamed us for ruining the relationship with him, as she showed us little to no affection. Her coping mechanism was food; she ate constantly, oblivious to her flabby body, becoming a mountain of a woman; and her size was intimidating.

With a home-life burdened with poverty, abuse and neglect, I turned to people at school for warmth, love and support. School was my escape from the chaos that haunted my home. Away from that horrible place, I pretended to be whoever I wanted to be. These flights of fancy are how I survived. I wore a paper mask, through which no one could see the real me. I was a good student and never drew negative attention to myself. This made me acceptable to peers and teachers alike. I blended in so well that no one knew about my home life. If they suspected anything, nobody let on.

One time my mother hit me across the face with a belt and gave me a black eye. She did not want me to go to school. I begged her to let me go and assured her I would lie about my black eye and they would never know how it really happened. We worked out a plan - I would tell my teacher that I hit my face on a shelf near my bed. School was my only happiness, the string of life that I gripped tightly. At school, I found adults on whom I could trust and rely. It was my sixth grade teacher who first took a particular interest in me and encouraged me to pour my energy into academics and strive for perfection. He gave me praise and hope for a better life. Maybe the "American Dream" was not such a fantasy after all. Reluctantly, mother let me go to school that day, black eye and all, and I stayed true to my word; I told nobody what had really happened.

Not long after the end of sixth grade, our home life became unbearable. I found myself unable to pretend anymore. To make matters worse, our father totally abandoned us, as he filed for divorce and left the home. That decision caused my mother's mental and physical health problems to increase rapidly. She was completely dependent on him and gladly accepted any scraps of affection he threw her way, but now he was gone and she was powerless to change it. She had lost the only man she ever loved, the only person that really mattered to her.

The idea of caring for six children on her own without him was unbearable for my mother. Worse then that, no matter where his job took him, and no matter whose bed he was sleeping in, he always came home to her. She depended on that tiny bit of stability. This time, though, she knew it was different. He was not coming home ever again. She was falling over the edge, tortured by his abandonment, so she escaped into the shadows of her mind. There were times she just sat on the couch for days awaiting his call. She would not eat, would not shower, and would not talk. She was almost comatose. He never called; he never came—not for her, not for us.

On Independence Day 1991, she shuffled us into the local domestic violence shelter where we spent the summer and a portion of the following school year. The domestic violence shelter was located outside of my school district. In compliance with the McKinney Vento Act, my school provided my siblings and me with special transportation accommodations to ensure that we stayed in the same school district. After time limits would no longer allow us to stay at the shelter, we returned to the empty house from which we had originally escaped.

Isolation and stress overcame my mother. A failed suicide attempt hospitalized her again and we entered out-of-home care. My siblings and I spent three months with a foster family while my mother underwent psychiatric lockdown.

Learning that I was going into foster care came as a terrible and unexpected shock. I was in history class when I received a note from the office instructing me to report to the principal's office at the end of the school day. When I arrived at the office, a social worker and my foster mother awaited me.

I still remember the social worker's words: "Your mom is sick, and she had to go to the hospital for help. She will be okay. You will see her as soon as she gets better."

When I asked about my siblings, my foster mother assured me that we would all be living with her. Although the idea of moving in with her was a shock, she was not a stranger. My foster mother knew my parents, and she knew me. She used to deliver USDA-FDA approved commodities to our home. I was always so excited when the box arrived that I eagerly tore it open looking for treats. We did not have treats very often. In fact, when school was not in session, our mother did not allow us to eat a lunch at home. Lunch was a luxury to which I looked forward and enjoyed during the school year. In foster care, we enjoyed three meals a day, even on weekends. My foster mother was a wonderful cook. Occasionally, she and her husband even took us to a restaurant, a treat that never happened when we lived with my mother.

In addition to regular meals, another bonus of foster care was being able to do crafts. My foster mother was a very creative person. One of the crafts I enjoyed most was when she purchased teddy bears for my sisters and me to make outfits. She taught us how to use a glue gun and we sewed aprons and skirts for the bears from pieces of material and lace. My foster parents also owned three dogs. We all took pleasure in playing with them. We had pets at home too, but they never lasted. The dogs we had were usually as neglected as we were. We could not afford to feed them and my mother did not have the interest or the discipline to ensure our animals were housebroken. Sadly, with tear stained dirty faces, we were forced to give up our pets shortly after they arrived and we had fallen in love with them.

My foster father was a nice man, but he was also very distant. It was as if he were afraid to form an attachment to us because he knew we would be leaving. He was a car mechanic, known throughout the neighborhood for his skills. He often spent time helping neighbors solve their car troubles. My foster father seemed more comfortable around my brothers, and let his wife work with us girls. He had one son from a previous marriage. His son was the same age and in the same grade as my older brother. My foster brother and my older brother were chums. My foster mother never had any children of her own. I believe becoming a foster parent filled that void in her life.

Some practices within the foster home were alien to us, and not always understood. My foster parents were devoted to their choice of religion. Our participation in their church took a tremendous amount of time. My siblings and I went from having no connection to church to attending three times a week. I felt that my foster parents believed attending church functions was more important than school. I didn't understand that. All too often, I was not able to complete homework assignments because of having to attend church functions two nights a week. My foster mother was strict about bedtime too, and she was reluctant to allow me to stay awake past bedtime to complete homework assignments. My grades fell, and I was devastated. My lifeline was threatened. Truthfully, that hurt me more than losing my parents. Pleasing my teachers meant everything to me.

After three months of intense psychiatric services, my mother's condition stabilized. We thought that signaled her cure and we were going home. Reunification with our mother occurred at the end of March 1992. Our case remained open and the caseworker continued to monitor our transition back into our home. The court ordered homemaker services, and my mother received in-home therapy.

Sadly, after a brief six-month period, my mother tried to end her life a second time and we children returned to our original foster family. My siblings and I were very lucky. We were all together, and in a familiar environment. Unfortunately, however, the huge amount of care the six of us needed took its toll on our foster parents. My foster mother took me aside and stated that she was no longer able to take care of us all. She felt that she and I had a good relationship, and she wanted to keep my older brother and me in her home. She didn't know anything about the placements of my four younger siblings. I was glad she wanted to keep us, but I also worried about the welfare of my younger siblings. Where would they go? Would they be okay? Would I get to see them? Just as quick as this conversation happened, things began to change . . . and fast.

It was becoming clear that my mother might never be in a position to care for us; her mental illness was becoming more severe, and it was more than she could handle just to take care of herself. The court made a serious effort to locate our father. Sixteen months had passed from the time my father left our family to the time the court contacted him directing that he reclaim us. We had not seen him in all this time. The court ordered reunification almost immediately.

Confused about how fast things were happening, I tried to make the best of it. In October 1992, I entered the eighth grade in a new school district. I took this opportunity to recreate myself. No one at this school knew from where I came or what had happened to me—or if they did, I did not know it. I transitioned easily into my new school, welcomed by both peers and teachers.

I was grateful that through this decision, my siblings and I were able to remain together. Our reunion was not without flaws, however. My father had a new significant other, and she was not pleased about taking in six children who were not her own. She had no problem expressing herself in front of us. She was not happy. It was a "duty" call. We were "excess baggage." She and I did not hit it off from the start. I refused to call her "Mom." After all, she was not my real mother, she was a stranger, and one I did not like. I just knew she stole our dad from us in the first place. She was a home wrecker. Later in life, though, I came to realize that it was easier to blame her than him.

With the heavy influx of six new mouths to feed, my father and his girlfriend faced a major reduction in the standard of living they enjoyed without us. As the years passed, our home literally eroded, and without funding to make necessary house repairs, living in the home became horrendous. Every spring when the sun melted the snow, my bedroom flooded. My father placed two by four boards across the floor so that my sisters and I could walk from our beds to our dressers without soaking our socks. Black mold crept up the walls like ivy, making us sick. We could not have friends over, either, although we would have been too embarrassed to have our friends see how we lived anyway.

I did not complain. Instead, I found refuge with friends who were happy to have me stay with them in their family homes. I adapted to this transient lifestyle well, and avoided going home as much as I could. My father never forced any of us to stay in the home, and we all found our own way to cope with the situation. No one reported to the child protective services office regarding the deplorable conditions of my father's home. Bad as it was, I had not for a second forgotten the beatings when we lived with my mother. Anything was better than living like that . . . anything.

Most states consider reunification successful if the placement remains stable for six months. If my worker had monitored my family for a year, he would have witnessed the flooding. Perhaps he could have provided our family with home weatherization assistance and spared us from living in these substandard conditions.

My biological father was physically and emotionally distant, as was my foster father. My child welfare caseworker, who was also male, I only saw a few times. I don't feel like he tried to get to know me. Much of his opinion about me developed from the opinions of my foster mother during their phone conversations. This compilation of negative experiences with men responsible for taking care of me and looking out for my best interest, would later lay the groundwork for my apprehension to trust or get close to men in my young adulthood.

Over the coming years, my gymnastics coach, a college professor and my husband-to-be were some of the people who entered my life and showed me that love does not always hurt. They taught me that I could believe in myself, and I could trust without being afraid of rejection or abandonment. They made me realize that I counted as a person just as much as anyone did. They gave me the freedom to learn about myself. I had skills I did not know I had.

I did not have to pretend anymore. Once I came to know myself, the real me, I discovered a secret: for the first time in my life, I liked me.

With high school graduation quickly approaching, I became afraid. School was my safety net. I knew that college was not an option for me, it was mandatory. I pushed myself forward, and with the assistance of several mentors, I went on to college. In graduate school, one of my professors turned out to be a foster care alumnus. He convinced me that having a foster care history would strengthen my career and should not be something from which to hide. I specialized in child welfare.

Upon graduation from Michigan State University, I secured a position with the Michigan Department of Human Services as a CPS worker. Initially I was afraid to take this position. What if I had a case that mirrored my own life story? Would I be able to deal with it? Would taking this job cause me to suffer post-traumatic stress disorder symptoms? Fortunately, the worries I initially had did not surface in reality. Instead, my experience proved the opposite of my initial concerns.

I believe that having a history of being a recipient of child welfare services enabled me to connect with and engage the youth on my caseload. Many of the parents I substantiated also happened to have been foster care alumni. I think that knowing I was a foster care alumnus gave them hope that being involved in the child welfare system did not have to seal their fate; that it was possible to overcome the challenges impeding their ability to parent effectively. Many of the families with whom I worked did not see me as the enemy, as Child Protective Service workers often are; instead, they regarded me as one of them, and someone who truly wanted to see them succeed.

I left Child Protective Services when I had the opportunity to split my workweek by working as a change agent with Michigan's Children, a children's advocacy agency specializing in legislative advocacy, and as a research specialist for the Michigan State University's School of Social Work. It has been a great honor and opportunity to work directly with policy makers and assist in making policy changes that will improve outcomes for youth in the foster care system.

In regards to my family—my terribly dysfunctional family is still dysfunctional when we are together, but each is working on going forward in his or her own way. I was lucky to have had wonderful mentors to help guide my way and they are still dear to my heart. It's sad to say the damage that occurred between our mother and us children was irreparable. However, we all have a relationship with our father.

The younger siblings, who either did not remember or did not experience the beatings because they were so young, often look at me with denial in their eyes when I speak about how our birth mother mistreated us older children. I have learned to accept that. They never walked in my shoes or those of my older brother's and for that, I am grateful. I will be even more grateful if none of my children shows hereditary signs of mental problems or an abusive nature.

Today, I am very happy, with a loving family of my own and a wonderful career. I would like to think I am living my own "American Dream." It was not easy, and at times, I really struggled, but with a little self-confidence, and the right help from compassionate people, we can all reach for our dreams. If through my own pain I can save just one child, then baring my soul is what I will do. My life has gone full circle . . . down a road paved with forgiveness.

The Degree of Caring

DANITA ECHOLS

I am the eldest of four children, African-American with light brown skin, a full figure and geeky glasses. My brother, who is less than a year younger than I am, is the color of dark chocolate and rail thin. We called my baby sister "Polar Bear" because she was fair skinned and plump. My youngest brother shares the same dark complexion as my other brother, but he was huskier as a child. I tell you this because size, shape and skin color have always been important to my family. There were long conversations about how fat someone was or how light or dark they were. By way of example, we referred to my grandmother's bosom as "Bunker Hill." In contrast, we called my mother's chest the "itty-bitty titty committee." Another example, my grandmother once smacked my sister's mouth after she said she had seen a bug as black as my grandmother's complexion.

My earliest memories start at age five, in my grandmother's basement, where we four children lived with my mother. Although this was not my first home and certainly not the last, I remember it best because it is where I learned parental roles, social norms and family secrets.

My mother was 22 years old, coffee-color skin, thin and pretty, with physical and mental health issues. She wore wigs and lots of makeup. Because she slept late, we children waited for her to get up or we fed ourselves. Sometimes we got out of bed early, snuck upstairs to eat one meal with my grandfather before he left for the plant, then a second meal with my aunt before she went to the post office and then a third meal with my grandmother, all before my mother awoke.

I have never seen documentation of my mother's mental health issues, but I do know that she spent time hospitalized as a child and adult because of her "episodes." I learned early to read my mother's moods. She might wake up and be a loving angel or a hateful devil, but she also could change from one to the other in the blink of an eye.

Her physical health is something of a mystery too, because other than asthma, there is no documentation of the chronic illnesses she claimed to suffer. We four children agreed with her siblings that she is a combination hypochondriac, kleptomaniac and schizophrenic. We came to our conclusion based on her behaviors and our understanding of the definition of the words. My mother taught us early on never to use a word unless we can spell and define it.

The doctors instructed my mother not to have children, due to her health. This medical advice fell on deaf ears. She stated that no one was going to keep her from having children, and family stories confirm that she had an affinity to run away with different men. My mother believed that she had to get pregnant before the doctors "sterilized" her. That is why she "settled" for my biological father.

My mother was a petite woman with a giant temper who fought dirty. She would use any item near her to strike out, a stick, coat hanger, belt, extension cord. I remember her threatening to hit me "until I cried." By age five, it took a lot to make me cry from her constant abuse. She even forced my brothers and sisters to watch her administer her cruel punishment. Although I refused to cry, I did feel the emotional pain of her not loving them or me enough. To make matters worse, other family members saw the marks and bruises, but did nothing to protect me from the beatings. As firstborn, I was the scapegoat for my mother's mental health issues.

I have no memory of the man who fathered me. When at age five I asked my mother about him, she told me he had died and I never asked about him again. I do remember my grandfather, though, a hard working alcoholic who married a tough woman in my grandmother. My grandmother ruled the roost, like an ill-tempered hen, and when my grandfather took exception to her pecking, there would be a confrontation, which often turned violent. My grandmother rarely fought alone; her children joined her in the assault. Once, after a particularly violent battle, I went upstairs to see blood everywhere: on the walls, floor, ceiling and broken doors. I heard the ambulance earlier and thought they had finally killed him, but he survived to fight another day.

My grandmother demanded the adoration of her family. She would pit her children and grandchildren against each other to win her favor. She seldom included my grandfather in anything. He slept alone on a twin bed in the far corner of her master bedroom. My grandmother's house was the one with plastic covering the living room furniture that only guests could sit on.

We did not attend church but my grandmother was big on gospel radio and television shows. I became interested in these activities too, probably to curry her favor. I learned the Bible stories and their meanings. The Bible, God and a life without pain captured my imagination. I wanted to be a part of this mystical Garden of Eden and to experience a life without suffering.

One day, after a particularly brutal beating from my mother, I was watching television when a commercial came on about children starving in Africa. My world had been so limited that the suffering of other children never occurred to me. That is when suicide first crossed my mind. I thought that maybe if I were dead I could get past the pain and discuss with God the discrepancies between what the Bible said and what several million children and I were experiencing. Everybody said that Heaven was a wonderful and peaceful place, and my unsophisticated six-year-old mind envisioned a life of no more beatings or worries about food, shelter, love and acceptance. I did not attempt suicide that day because I questioned who, if I were gone, would take care of my siblings and my mother. The struggle not to end my life continued for the next 30 years, though.

Because their selfish personalities clashed, my mother was never able to stay with my grandmother very long, so we moved a lot. I quickly learned not to get used to anything because it could change in an instant. We stayed in hotels, motels, the Salvation Army (before they had family shelters) and with the many fictive kin whom mother managed to beguile.

Our fictive kin were often just ordinary people who cared about children. Big Auntie, for example, was a single mom who took on the responsibility of helping raise other people's kids. She operated a deli in which all of us worked to earn our keep. She had a few quirks, like expecting immediate action to her demands, but she also looked out for us when we ran away from my mother or needed something to eat. Distorted as my sense of family was during those early years, Big Auntie and several others helped me to develop a more healthy understanding of what a family should be.

I do not know why my mother decided to discuss sex with us at such an early age. I choose to believe she did so because we sometimes stayed in dangerous places. She told us sickening tales of rape and sodomy and provided pornographic images to ensure that we knew what could happen. Although I never experienced rape, I did spend many sleepless nights worrying about the safety of my siblings. My sister and brothers seemed to fascinate perverts. Great uncles wanted to be alone with them, fictive kin talked about things they thought we did not understand and some females even wanted to give my brothers baths.

Finally, when I turned seven, the court put my siblings and me in foster care. I am sure the authorities gave little thought to placing us with grandmother because the prevailing social work philosophy of the early 1970s dictated that the apple did not fall far from the tree and, therefore, the relatives were just as likely to have problems.

The court placed me in the home of a black minister and his wife. They also had an adult daughter and another foster child in the home. To my surprise, this was a male dominated household. Both the wife and daughter obeyed the man. I had no prior experience of a man heading the family.

We went to church all day Sunday and at least twice during the week. I was an outspoken youth who questioned Bible School and the lessons taught there. I wanted to know who wrote the Bible and why there were so many different interpretations of its meaning. The minister did his best to assist in my understanding religion. In retrospect, I am amazed at how patiently he tried to answer the questions of a seven-year-old who, in turn, questioned his answers and had no fear of pain or punishment. Indeed, I now courted pain.

Since I was no longer suffering abuse, I began to perform self-mutilation. I know it sounds crazy, but physical pain had a prominent place in my life during my formative years, and without it, it was almost as if I were no longer alive or in touch with my feelings. The pain was all I had left of my family, and I missed them, especially my brothers and sister, so, to remind myself of them, I would cut or scrape myself to cause a scab, and then pull the skin off, one layer at a time. If that did not suffice, I stuck pins in my hands or feet, anything that helped me stay in touch with them, so painful were my separation feelings.

I could not believe that I was now living in a family that did not have secrets. I watched, waited, poked and prodded, but found nothing amiss in this household. Instead, there was laughter, shared work, consistency and responsibility. As the youngest, I did not have chores to perform, other than to make my bed. Instead, I could go outside and play, just as my younger siblings had, when we lived together. Everything began coming together. For the first time in my brief but stress-filled life, I lowered my defenses and embraced the positive emotions this stable, loving family provided. Then, the moment I finally stopped missing my brothers and sister and started to adjust to this new way of living, it came to a screeching halt.

My three siblings and I returned to my mother's care without benefit of an explanation or support services. We shared our placement experiences. My sister had lived with a white family. She blocked out most of her memories of this time, her coping mechanism most of her life. My two brothers lived with a black family, but never felt comfortable in their placement. Now back with our mother, danger, uncertainty, abuse and neglect returned to our young lives, but we did not care about any of that, because we were together again, and family life as we knew it had returned to the norm.

Our next foster care placement came within a few months of returning to the care of my mother. I was now eight years old and we lived in an inner-city basement apartment. Mother had left me with the food stamps, a handgun and orders not to let anyone in. I would leave the apartment with my brother to get food and then return quickly and quietly. The apartment building was dangerous. Pimps, prostitutes and junkies populated it. We often heard gunfire, beatings, screams and crying. We lived in fear of our lives and did our best to be as quiet as church mice for fear that someone might break in and kill us.

One day the police came. Some concerned citizen called them because we were not attending school and no one had seen my mother in over a week. When the police knocked on the door, we did not answer. We knew better. I remember how still we became, like living statues frozen in place, and that we held our breath for what seemed forever. When the police stated who they were, I told them how my mother had instructed me not to open the door for anyone but her. The police threatened to kick the door in, and if memory serves me, that's when I told them I had a loaded gun aimed at the door. I do not remember how they got into the apartment, but I do know they took the gun from my hand, carefully, so as not to hurt me or discharge a round. We were frightened and confused as they drove us to the police station, sirens blasting.

They placed us in D. J. Healey, a shelter. The best part of the shelter for me was that this time the four of us remained together. I lived in the girls' cottage with my sister and my brothers stayed in the boys' cottage across the yard. The experience was good for me in some ways, because I got to be a kid again and did not have the responsibility of watching over and cleaning up after my younger siblings. I could relax, but only for a short while, because, once again, we returned to the care of our mother.

When we again moved back with my mother, nothing had really changed with her. There was always some drama playing out with her friends, lovers or neighbors. She dreamed up bizarre conspiracy theories, and even believed that God was out to get her. Her contact with reality continued to slip further and further away, and during those times when she forgot she had children, I did whatever I wanted to do. For example, I missed an entire year of elementary school and got into the habit of staying up all night.

For the next few years, we bounced from one foster home to another or back to our mother for a short while. Finally, just prior to my teens, the court placed us with Catholic Social Service. They, in turn, matched us with a family that had children of their own, but still took in all four of us. The family had some religious issues that included praying over us and then waiting for the demons to come out. They even dropped us off for several days with an old blind woman who had a rodent problem. She sprinkled rat poison on everything in the house, including the candy she kept out. Like most kids, when we saw the candy lying about, we ate it. Even though she knew we were sick from eating the candy, she did not call a doctor or have us taken to the hospital. Instead, she prayed over us, until the family finally came to pick us up. Although I do not know this as fact, it seemed that the foster parents were trying to hide us until they received payment from Catholic Social Services. We never saw a counselor or social worker the entire time we lived with them.

During other placements, however, I did take tests and met with counselors and social workers. I sometimes think I was the guinea pig for all of the white, suburban, fresh-out-of-college counselors and social workers. I quickly grew bored taking their tests and answering their questions so I sometimes made up stuff—silly stuff—to test them in return. They did not seem sincerely interested in me, and I felt likewise about them. Seldom did I see the same counselor or social worker more than twice, so we had no real rapport built on trust over time.

On one of the many occasions the court removed us from our mother's care, there was no foster home to place us. We spent the first night at 801 Baltimore Street, the main Children's Services Office in Detroit. The decrepit, bug-infested building had no beds for us to sleep on and no food to eat, and it was creepier than any foster home. The next day, they transferred us to the juvenile detention facility. Although we stayed there only briefly, I will never forget how abandoned I felt, as no one seemed to care what happened to my siblings and me. Despite doing nothing wrong, we received the same treatment as hardened juvenile delinquents.

After a time we were placed in grandmother's custody. She had separated from my grandfather and now lived with her youngest son. We had nowhere to sleep in this two-bedroom house except on the floor because someone else rented the upstairs. We four children eventually did sleep upstairs, but by then I was a teenager and no longer comfortable with my brothers being in the same room with me.

In the beginning, the drama at my grandmother's new home was less than before, but she still had favorites and scapegoats, and it was difficult not to become part of the constant competition for her attention or that of others. All of my siblings were someone's favorite, either blood relatives or fictive kin, which included men who could have been the biological father to some of my siblings. As for me, I faded into the background, staying alert for signs that it was time to pack our bags, hoard food or protect my sister and brothers.

I had a reputation for a bad temper, especially if someone bothered my siblings. I fought often, sometimes with more than one person, and I seldom lost. I had that much anger inside me, and I was afraid of what my mother or grandmother would do if I lost. They taught me to fight dirty and win at all costs, which is why I carried salt and pepper with me to blind my opponents in a fight.

School was my solace. I enjoyed learning. Learning was always easy for me, that is, until I went to Renaissance High School. Renaissance was a new magnet school in Detroit when I started in the second half of 9th grade. School then became a challenge. I went from the honor roll to struggling to maintain a C average. I found myself competing with other smart kids who knew how to study and who worked hard for their grades. I had minimal study skills and even less self-discipline. My grades slipped, but I learned from my mother that if I used the "poor foster child" routine, the school would probably help me. My mother knew all about manipulation, a skill she had learned from my grandmother, and now it was part of my culture.

Living with my grandmother returned to the dramatic and traumatic existence I had known years before when we lived in her basement. She could be just as violent with us as my mother was. She expected me to perform the many duties I had when I lived with my mother, except handle money—she controlled that. I cleaned, cooked and became her scapegoat. I could no longer protect my siblings from beatings. My grandmother used the same weapons as my mother did when it came to administering physical punishment. For example, one time when my brother did not move fast enough for her, my grandmother hit him over the head with a frozen 10-pound tube of hamburger, knocking him down. That pushed me over the edge. I could not take it anymore. The next day, I burst into tears during class and then reported the incident to my teacher. The court moved me out of the house, but left my sister and brothers with my grandmother. I spent the next several years trying to make it up to my siblings for leaving them, so deep was my sense of guilt.

This time, I went to Defer, a girls' home named after the street. Because it made the agency look good, I continued to attend Renaissance High School, even though it was across town from Defer. I took two buses to school and three buses to get back, doing my homework on the bus trips, and returning to Defer near twilight, exhausted. My nickname at Defer was "Bookworm."

Someone must have heard me grumbling about living on the east side of Detroit and attending school on the west side because they transferred me to Marlowe House, near Renaissance High. Marlowe House was just like Defer, but with fewer girls. For the next two years, I attended classes at Renaissance and spent the summers working for minimum wage through a city job program, where I earned $800. I thought I was rich, until I learned that I was to save the money until I left the program. Leaving custody never crossed my mind. I mean, if I graduated high school what would I do? Where would I live? Who would pay my rent and electric bill, buy my food and purchase my clothes? I had adjusted so well to being part of the child social welfare system that I could no longer comprehend taking care of myself.

I turned 18 in March and sought immediate release from foster care, but the Department of Social Services and Marlowe House refused. I was to remain in care until I graduated from high school. I had no independent living skills. The system did not provide independent living classes and I had forgotten the few skills I had prior to foster care. While living with my mother, I was in charge of grocery shopping, cooking, cleaning and balancing the checkbook, but I had not lived with my mother and held that level of responsibility for years. It is a good thing that they pushed me to graduate because I started to panic about independent living and received my first failing grade, an F in calculus. Nonetheless, I graduated that June.

I thought my family would be proud of me and attend graduation. I gave them all invitations. They patted me on the back and told me how proud they were of me, adding that they would be there to watch me cross the stage and receive my diploma. As always, though, my family was more about making promises than keeping them. Not one of them came to acknowledge my passage from student to graduate, child to adult. It was just another anticlimactic moment in my life, another letdown, one more denial of those significant events enjoyed by "normal" kids, such as prom pictures, the senior class trip, a class ring, a graduation gift. I stood there in the middle of the auditorium, conspicuously alone, wearing my prettiest dress and forcing my widest smile, while adoring families kissed, hugged and congratulated my classmates. On the most significant day of my young life, I wanted to die, to fade away, so ashamed was I that no one cherished me.

Self-pity gave way to worry about where to live. Graduation brought with it emancipation, which meant I could no longer live at Marlowe House and I no longer qualified for Department of Social Services assistance. After years as a ward of the state, the social services support systems I had come to rely on abruptly vanished, totally, forever. The Department of Social Services was no longer my parent after 11 years. I had not a clue how unprepared I was for independence, especially since I could not count on either the foster care system or my family to help me bridge this difficult transition.

Naiveté is a wonderful thing. So is luck. I left Marlowe House with savings of $800. I knew nothing about paying for my own living expenses after three years of residential care. Fortunately, one of my aunts let me stay with her for the summer, delaying my need to learn responsibility. By the end of summer, I had spent ever penny of that $800. That was okay, though, I rationalized, because I would soon begin a work-study job at Eastern Michigan University.

Unfortunately, I was unprepared for the freedom and the responsibility of college life. Years of relying on other people to tell me what to do failed to teach me personal skills such as self-reliance and self-motivation. Instead of getting up early and attending my eight o'clock classes, for example, I did what I wanted to do, which was to sleep late and skip class. I partied, shopped and spent my work-study check as soon as I got it. The reckoning came at the end of my first semester at Eastern Michigan. I failed all of my subjects due to lack of attendance and I owed the university money because I misspent my work-study checks on self-indulgences rather than paying my tuition.

What was I to do? I could no longer live in campus housing or attend classes, so I asked family for help. They refused me a place to stay or money for tuition. I contacted Marlowe House, but no one there could help me either. At age 18, I was entirely on my own, without benefit of family or social services to help me recover from my mistakes or point me in the right direction. A casual friend suggested that I beg my way back into Eastern Michigan by informing them that I had been in foster care and had no place to live. A sympathetic administrator suggested that I take out a student loan, which I did. After pleading and reassuring, I convinced the administration that I would buckle-down and be a better student. I was too, at least that semester, but beside financial and emotional support, I lacked the ambition, the passion, and the inner-drive, indeed, the maturity to earn a college education at this point in my young and still traumatized life.

For much of the next decade, I drifted aimlessly, copying my mother's history of living for the moment and constantly moving from one place to the next, one job to another, a life without purpose or direction. Everything about my life was temporary: work, apartments, roommates, acquaintances, interests. My meager belongings stayed in storage and I could move from one setting to another in less than three hours. I had learned from my family and foster care experiences to avoid attachments, as life was a series of random and temporal events over which I had little control.

Fortunately, as I grew older, my emotional maturity began to catch up to my chronological age, presenting me with a life-changing opportunity. I was in my mid-twenties and employed as a food service worker at the University of Michigan, when I learned of the Women of Color Conference on campus and met an amazing woman named Germaine Key. She asked me what I did for a living. I told her that I worked for the University of Michigan, but that I also helped HIV/AIDS patients, volunteered with the Ann Arbor welfare rights organization and mentored a foster child. Ms. Key explained that if I worked in the foster care system, I could use my experiences in foster care to help improve the lives of many other foster children.

That is when I knew I wanted to be a social worker. I could reflect on my own past to understand the needs of foster children and perhaps develop appropriate programs, policies and procedures and advocate on their behalf. Maybe this was the reason for my dysfunctional childhood, I thought, and perhaps my purpose was to help make a better life for other foster kids. Shortly thereafter, I quit my job at UM and matriculated back to Eastern Michigan University, where I spent two years as a social work student and employee at the Institute for the Study of Children and Families.

The Institute provided opportunities to work with and learn from child welfare professionals. Immersed in a learning culture where students and faculty embraced similar goals, my life now had purpose. The Directors of the Institute nurtured me from a neophyte in child welfare policy to a mature and knowledgeable childcare professional and promoted my passion to improve foster care. I earned a Bachelor of Social Work from Eastern Michigan University in December 1992.

Armed with my BSW degree and high hopes for improving the lives of foster children, I accepted my first professional child welfare position in Philadelphia, Pennsylvania. Unfortunately, however, academic theory and personal altruism quickly collided with abject reality. I soon learned that the term "social worker" is more a misnomer than an accurate description of job function. Indeed, I spent far more of my time in the roles of a "desk jockey" and "paper pusher" than I did working with children, their biological families or foster families. The agency and my co-workers showed no interest in building relationships with their clients. Crushed by the reality that the "professionals" charged with serving the "best interest of the child" barely knew, indeed, maybe never met the children they represented or the foster families to whom they were assigned prompted me to question my employment. After 13 months working at this agency, I tendered my resignation.

I returned to Michigan disheartened and disillusioned, but still dedicated to the belief that I could make a difference in the lives of foster children. The Philadelphia experience had to be an aberration, I rationalized, but, sadly, as I have learned over the past 14 years, it was not. I have held state and private agency social work positions, all of which have fallen woefully short of my ideal. I even went back to school to learn more about "best practices" and research related to improving the lives of foster children, earning a Master of Social Work from Wayne State University in May 1998.

Superiors, colleagues and co-workers in foster care sometimes accuse me of being "too invested" in helping foster kids. They say that I am apt to "believe the kids too much" and that I cannot "save every child." I say baloney! I say that every child needs, no, deserves all the help I can muster on their behalf. That is my job. That is my mission. Isn't that what social work is supposedly about?

Certainly, I admit to my personal crusade to help foster children. How could I not do what I do without being deeply committed to doing my best? I understand the emotional pain and psychological confusion these young people endure, and I know that doing my best can make all the difference to a child who has no voice but through me. That is why I am "too invested." That is why I "believe the kids too much." That is why I strive to "save every child." That is what is required.

Having spent most of my life as a foster care client, student or professional, I must admit to sometimes feeling frustrated by the poor services still provided to foster children. I read about blue ribbon panels of "experts" who impart their recommendations for improvement, but little, if anything, really changes for the betterment of foster kids. These so-called "experts" tend to repeat the same misinformed policies and procedures espoused by their predecessors. They seldom provide innovation, such as including the voices of former foster kids on their blue ribbon panels or on the boards of directors of agencies and organizations serving foster kids. How can they know how to meet our needs if they have not walked in our shoes?

When discussing my frustration about the foster care system with a fellow social worker, she described the gulf between my ideal of providing foster care services and that of other social workers who have not shared my experiences as "the degree of caring." She went on to explain that I might risk my life to jump in front of a moving bus to push a foster child to safety, while other social workers might only yell for the youth to move. If that is the case, then those social workers should seek employment elsewhere. Helping these vulnerable young people survive the foster care system must be much more than a job, it must be a mission; otherwise, "the degree of caring" will always be lacking.

The "degree of caring" relates to how the foster care system delivers services, too. For example, foster care workers may have degrees in human services but they spend little time actually performing social work. Instead, they are busier filling out paperwork and conducting other bureaucratic chores than working directly with foster children and their families. To do actual "social work" requires working after hours, on your own time and, often, in secret. Consequently, it is difficult for foster care workers to provide their clients the help they need with such mundane tasks as searching for a job, filling out an application, balancing a checkbook, applying to college, seeking health care or understanding their needs. Actually spending time with foster children, their relatives or foster parents can be the crucial difference between just moving these already disconnected children from one placement to the next and helping them to form permanent bonds. From my experience, every time a foster child gets a new social worker, moves from one residential setting to another or suffers abuse in care, it diminishes their ability to transition from dependent child to independent adult. Already disenfranchised by their own families, they also endure deprivation by the support systems whose "mission" it is to protect, nourish and guide them, both during and after foster care. Is it any wonder, then, that so many of us end up on the streets, addicted to drugs, pregnant, unemployed, in jail or prison?

Emancipation from foster care is equivalent to throwing an 18-year-old into the ocean without benefit of swimming lessons or a life raft. Getting safely back to shore becomes more about luck than ability. Indeed, youth aging out of care need just as much - if not more support - than do the youth in care. Recognizing the individual needs of youth leaving foster care and the deficits of not having a support system are paramount to bringing these youth into the social norm. Current policy is cookie cutter and leaves little room for individual circumstances, human error or personal frailties. Few foster youth are prepared for independent living, but <u>all</u> foster youth must be perfect the first time they venture out on their own. They do not have the benefit of family to serve as swimming instructors or lifeguards. Rather, it is the responsibility of the systems and professionals charged with the welfare of foster children to emulate "the degree of care" provided by a loving family, both during childhood and into early adulthood. Anything less can never suffice. Prove my coworker wrong by being willing to risk your own safety to push the child from in front of the bus. Such is "the degree of care" required to make a positive difference in the lives of this vulnerable population of disconnected, scared and scarred youth whose outcome relies on the system of professionals whose mission it is to protect and advocate for them, as they would for their own children.

Dark Past, Bright Future:
Growing Past Family Violence, Neglect and Abandonment

≈⊛≈

MAURICE WEBB

A blizzard of mid-winter Michigan sleet and snow pelted my mother and me as we pressed forward, my little hand clinging to hers, winding our way around piles of freshly plowed snow and across icy-slick sidewalks to nursery school, my first day. I was three years old and both excited and anxious to start nursery school and make friends with my new classmates. My only concern was separating from my mother when she dropped me off, but she promised to return and fetch me back home because she kept repeating in her most soothing mommy voice: "Don't worry, Maurice, the time will fly by and then I'll be back to pick you up before you know it." She returned for me that afternoon, as promised, but my life thereafter seemed stuck in that cold gray day, as my developing mind began to process what was happening in our home.

My father never took me to school or, for that matter, did anything to tend me. He made it clear that it was my mother's job to look after my needs. "That's woman's work!" he would scold my mother, when she asked him to do something on my behalf or for anyone else, for that matter. Everything was all about him, as though my mother and I were merely there to please him. He was a mean man, given to violence, both physical and verbal, and my mother felt the brunt of his abuse all too frequently. He would slam her to the floor and she'd scream so loud that my head ached from the ringing of her frightened cries for help: "Mark! Mark! Little Mark! Come get him off me!" She always called me Mark instead of Maurice when she needed my help, which was often.

I would run to the living room or kitchen or wherever he sat astride her to witness the abuse while it happened. There he was, this huge man holding down my much smaller mother with his full weight on her chest and knees clamped down on her arms, while she squirmed and kicked at him and screamed for my help. I pleaded with him to leave my mother alone: "Stop it, Daddy! Stop it! Please stop it, Daddy, you're hurting her!" Then I would break down, sobbing as my little body convulsed with fear and confusion, knowing that it was not normal for daddies and mommies to hurt each other.

My father would attempt to explain to me that it was always my mother's fault and that he was just trying to restrain her, as if I were stupid enough to believe him. Of course, it never started like that, though. Most of the time, it began when they drank too much alcohol. They would pass the bottle between them—laughing and joking - but before long, they would begin arguing in a drunken stupor and then, after a few more swigs, a fight ensued. I had no idea what alcohol did to a person; I mistakenly thought it was what adults did to have fun.

As I grew older, I began to disassociate myself from what was happening between my parents. I imagined that I did not really exist, that I was some kind of a phantom, a ghost or a spirit that was not part of this world or that family. I know now that my attempt at mental escape was a defense mechanism used to insulate me from the cruelty that tortured my emotions. At that time in my early childhood, however, when he hit her again and again, I couldn't help but think to myself how he was destroying the only person who truly loved me. I knew my mother loved me because she walked me all the way to and from school every day, regardless of the weather. Only someone who loved me would make such a sacrifice.

The beatings got so bad that my mother and I ran off to shelters to escape the abuse. I remember thinking to myself that we should stay there until he died; then we could go back to a normal life, although I had no idea what a "normal" life was. Sadly, though, she always went back to him. Don't ask me why. Maybe she wanted to be there when he died so that she could help him have a good death. Perhaps she had it in her mind to watch him die painfully. I guess—maybe—she actually did love him. Imagine that! Whatever the reason, it didn't matter to me, I just knew that he was the cause of our problems, and in order for my life to be better he had to die.

During the in-between times while I awaited my father's death, my mother and I moved around a lot. One time we lived with nine people in this rickety old house with beat-up furniture and no heat. Sometimes the house was so cold that we had to sleep in our coats, huddled close together. The bathroom smelled like a cesspool. The adults wore raggedy clothes, their eyes empty, searching for a fix. I never had so much as a bed or dresser to use while we lived there. We were just passing through, on our way to God knows where. My mother and I were gypsies, sometimes living with my father and other times staying in shelters or with my mother's family or friends.

Sometimes, my half-brother Khalil Bennett came to live with us, whenever his mother grew tired of him. Since we were born only three months apart, brothers from the same father but different mothers, we never thought of ourselves as half-brothers; we considered ourselves blood brothers. Khalil and I got along great most of the time, at least until we talked about our mothers. We both realized our mothers were seriously flawed. He knew my mother was a crackhead and I knew his mom mistreated and neglected him. I guess that made us even, sharing an abusive father and having screwed up mothers.

Khalil always got into fights and manipulated people for his own gain. I was shy and sensitive and probably naïve compared to him. One time, he sold my bike and gave away pop and candy bought with the proceeds, just to be friends with the popular kids in the neighborhood. Khalil and I shared a unique bond, we were always at odds but we also were best friends who shared many laughs together. Through thick and thin, we spent most of our childhood and teen years together.

School became my favorite place, not because I enjoyed learning history and math or valued the camaraderie of my classmates, but because they served breakfast and lunch. School was the only place I could count on for a square meal. The refrigerator at home when we lived with my father held more beer and wine than groceries, and meals were catch as catch can when we lived in a shelter or with friends. One time, when I knew there was no food for supper, Khalil and I hopped a neighbor's fence and stole as many green tomatoes as our greedy arms could cradle. Fried green tomatoes battered in corn meal is still one of my favorite foods.

The absence of regular meals took a back seat to the constant presence of my father's abusiveness. In the summer of 1994, my father and uncle got into a fight. They fought in the street for what seemed like hours, while the neighbors cheered them on as though it was a pay-per-view boxing match. After beating my mother's brother within an inch of his life, my father strode into the house like a victorious gladiator anticipating the praise of the mob in the Coliseum, his self-absorbed smirk symbolizing his pride in adding another notch to his belt. He gloried in his fighting abilities and expected me to take pride in him because he beat up another man. Instead of feeling pride, I cursed his existence and hoped that someday someone would beat him to death.

Living with my father became so unpredictable and violent that my mother and I spent a few weeks in protective custody. I vividly remember Halloween night 1996 just before midnight. After returning home from a festival in downtown Detroit, I witnessed one of the scariest moments of my young life. That day changed all of our family's lives forever. My grandmother on my mother's side of the family had died six months prior, leaving her flat to my mother and her brother. We took the downstairs apartment and my uncle took the upstairs apartment. This was, at best, a tenuous situation, given the still-simmering feud between my father and uncle. October 1996, two years from their last fight, my uncle knocked on the door of our apartment. He had finally had it with the havoc my father and mother created when they drank, argued or fought. My father opened the front door, my uncle called him out, and the next thing I heard was a bang, followed by a boom and a thud, and then another bang. I ran into the living room to witness my father and my uncle once again fighting like wild animals on the landing outside the front door.

My mother ran up behind me, panicking, as nervous energy spurred by fear shot her up the stairs and back down again, as if searching for some way to break up the fight. She kept calling my name, as she had so many times before when my father accosted her: "Mark! Mark! Get them to stop! Somebody, please do something!" However, unlike the last fight, no audience assembled to witness their private war or to stop it.

The next thing I knew, my uncle's 350-pound son lumbered from the back yard and teamed up against my father. He made matters only worse, getting as his reward for intervention, a bloody lip and swollen eye. The fracas finally ended in more of a whimper than a winner, as the combatants collapsed from exhaustion, too tired to utter another expletive or throw one more punch. They just lay there for a while, gasping for air, sweating and bleeding all over the place, mortal enemies dividing our family further apart. Just what happened to initiate their war still escapes me, although I suspect that my uncle thought he was somehow defending his sister or getting even for the beatings my father meted out to her. Sleep escaped me that night. We never set foot on that property again.

We moved to the west side of Detroit. Living on the west side of Detroit turned out worse than when we lived on the east side. We had no water, no heat and little or no food to eat. Much of the time, we subsisted on welfare and government-issued cheese. I hated the way we lived, in abject poverty, my parents drunk or stoned most of the time, the two of them caught up in a love-hate relationship that emphasized cruelty and escapism over compassion and reality. It was too much for my young mind to bear.

That is when I realized I had to take charge of my life. Neither my mother nor my father was capable of improving the way we lived. I could no longer take the snubs from classmates, who avoided me because my clothing stunk from lack of washing. I hated living on public assistance in squalid surroundings, begging other students to share their lunch. Things that most people considered necessary, I thought were luxuries.

I knew my mother and father cared little about my well-being and that if I had any chance at making it I had to do it myself. Selling drugs was not an option, as I saw what drugs did to those who used them and, besides, that was illegal, a one-way ticket to the pokey, and I wasn't about to go there. Nice clothes, fancy shoes and regular meals appealed to me, so in eighth grade I landed a part-time job after school and weekends at the local super market making $80.00 a week, before Uncle Sam took his bite. I could now buy my own clothing, shoes and food and maybe even fit in at school. I tried to save some of my paycheck, but my father took $20.00 a week for board. After buying school clothing and food, I had nothing left, and what little remained my father grabbed up, stating, "We'll just save this for your junior prom." I welcomed overtime because that little bit extra allowed me to purchase deodorant, toothpaste, soap and other necessities. Oh, and I never did see the junior prom money.

My family life grew more tumultuous with each passing day. The next two years nearly destroyed me. I had to cross the street to a neighbor's house and use their water hose to fill a bucket, bring it back home, boil it on the stove and take a kitchen shower. I got tired of that routine and began staying with my cousin—until I wore out my welcome. I nearly froze to death that winter, in that horrible place with no running water or heat.

Around this time, my mother got a night job and although she generally quit her jobs upon receiving her first paycheck, she actually kept this job for a while. One particular night changed our lives forever, when she returned home early and without cab fare. It was the same night I came home from staying with my cousin to find my father receiving oral sex from a woman. Since my mother did not have the money to pay the cabby, she asked my father to pay him. My father refused, forcing my mother to leave her State ID with the cab driver until she could pay him.

The whole scene made my blood boil. How could my father treat my mother so badly when she was bringing home the bacon, while he laid around unemployed and receiving oral sex from a stranger in our home? I told my mother what was going on while she was at work, and she stormed through the house looking for that woman. The next thing I knew, I heard my mother's voice cussing out that woman, who ran screaming from the bedroom and out into the street, half-dressed and shoeless.

Instead of accepting blame for his wrongdoing, my father turned his wrath on me by shoving me into the bathroom and wrapping his huge, meaty hands around my neck. He pressed so hard that I could not breathe or exhale. His 300-pound frame kept me pinned, my life ebbing from me, when out of the corner of my eye I glimpsed my mother bashing his head with a broom handle. He released me just as I was about to pass out, using his hands now to fend off the broom handle, which my mother rained down on him hard, rapidly and without forgiveness. This time, their roles reversed, she was the one giving the butt whipping and he was the one begging her to stop. I prayed she would kill him then and there.

Violence seemed our constant companion, not just at home, but on the streets, too. By my fourteenth birthday, our house had been fire-bombed and my mother wounded in a drive-by shooting. The final straw came when the Red Cross funding ran out and we had no choice but to return to our burned-out house. We had nothing left, no money: no friends, no family, nothing. My father had used up our money on booze and drugs, and he had spoiled all of our relationships. Our one remaining option was to return to a place where we had to sleep in coats—again. The chill wind ripped through our burned-out house. The fire department had cut a huge hole in its frame to put out the fire. We had no front door either; the police had kicked it in the week before because of a domestic violence report against my father. Only long pieces of clear plastic nailed to the front door and the hole in the frame of the house protected us from the chill of night and the danger of intruders. We had hit rock bottom.

I finally had enough. My father's behavior had taken everything from us. He had destroyed everything he touched, including our family. I wanted him dead more than ever. I dreamt up scenarios of his suffering a horrible death and then descending to Hell, where the Devil abused him for eternity. Oh, how I wanted him out of our lives.

The anguish continued when my mother and father just up and vanished one day, leaving Khalil and me to fend for ourselves, as Khalil was staying with us at that time. We had $15 between us. I knew my grandfather loved us enough to take us in, so we went there. We lived with him three months without hearing a word from my father or mother. I worked tirelessly at Wendy's restaurant flipping burgers while Khalil sold drugs for the neighborhood pushers.

The additional strain of trying to parent two rowdy teenagers affected my grandfather's already poor health, forcing him to contact Child Protective Services for help. Within a day or two of my grandfather's call to CPS, my father phoned advising that Child Protective Services had taken Khalil into custody and if I did not want to go into a group home, I should not return to my grandfather's house. With no place left to go, I spent the next four nights sleeping in abandoned buildings and alleyways until I finally turned myself into the court.

Only a few days prior to our grandfather's call to CPS, Khalil and I did something stupid. We stole a car and took it for a joyride, until the cops caught us, ending the joy part of the ride. We landed in juvenile court, where the judge adjudicated Khalil but gave me a second chance, stating that if I turned my life around, got good grades in school and stayed out of trouble, she would drop the delinquency charges. I heeded her advice and promised myself that I would walk the straight and narrow path from then on.

In January of 2000, the court placed us in foster care while deciding our fate. We should have been there much sooner. Perhaps our lives would have been better had the courts intervened years earlier and removed us from our dysfunctional parents.

Because of Khalil's criminal past and school truancy, the court placed him in a group home with intensive security measures. He remained there until he aged out of the system at 18.

My group home placement proved less than positive. The program operated on favoritism, inconsistency, insensitivity and improper supervision. Staff provided residents little or no support or guidance. I doubt they had any training in how to meet the special needs of foster children. It was as if the state were doing its civic duty by providing food and shelter for us, while the staff showed up to collect a paycheck.

The staff had no confidence in me. I can still hear the conversation of two staff talking about how they believed I would fail the program and end up in jail like many of the other kids. Thank God, I did not take their negative appraisal of me to heart and allow it to drag me down. I did not fail the program, go AWOL or land in jail. Rather, I went on to be the youngest person to graduate PIL (Pre-Independent Living Program), maintaining a 3.7 grade point average that year and winning the Youth of the Month Award three times. This taught me that I am capable of achieving anything I put my mind to. I also learned that adversity promotes growth and, perhaps more importantly, that adults should guard their words carefully when discussing vulnerable young people.

My social worker in PIL was Ms. Jones, who took special interest in me. After a few months in the group home, she decided to be my foster parent and took me to her home to live with her, which, according to state regulations, constitutes a conflict of interest. She lost her contract at PIL immediately.

The summer of my sixteenth birthday, I had finally found what I believed was a stable and loving home environment. Ms. Jones' house was clean and furnished neatly, had heat, air conditioning, running hot and cold water, a well-manicured lawn, a clean and safe neighborhood and kind and friendly neighbors. I attended a new high school where the other students accepted me, and I no longer had to worry about where my next meal would come from or be concerned about wearing unclean clothes to school. I thought I had died and gone to Heaven.

I also met a girl named Tina Lawrence, the most beautiful and wonderful girl I had ever known. I saw her at church, the mall and school. We even went on a college tour together. She initiated our relationship, although at the time I did not know why. My self-confidence was nearly nonexistent at that time. Maybe she saw something in me that I did not see in myself. What I did know was that I had fallen in love with her, deeply, and that her tenderness replaced the pain of my abusive and neglectful past with the emotional security for which I so longed. Tina taught me about affection, tenderness, sensitivity, selflessness and other positive feelings that people who care about each other share without hesitation or reservation. Such emotions were not part of my experience, as my own father and mother modeled an entirely different set of behaviors. Our relationship blossomed, as did I.

Tina's parents were the opposite of my mother and father. Instead of abuse and escapism, the Lawrence family emphasized love and communication, and rather than turning to alcohol or other drugs, they gloried in God and His guidance. They were wonderful people, the kind of "normal" black family I dreamed about but did not know existed, a working father and mother with four kids and an endless supply of love. Acceptance by Tina and her family provided a pivotal opportunity to feel a part of something beautiful at a time when my future seemed dim and pointless.

While my relationship with Tina and her family flourished, Ms. Jones and I grew steadily apart. She became increasingly punitive and cursed me constantly. Minor things about me seemed to set her off, such as forgetting a chore or breaking one of her many rules. Sometimes I spent weeks, even months, paying for my indiscretions. I didn't know why she changed her attitude toward me. Our relationship became so strained that I ran away twice to escape her wrath.

I failed the ACT, scoring only a 13. Ms. Jones warned me not to take it again, but I did take it a second time. I had made passing the ACT a goal because I wanted to attend college. Other people cheered me on, teachers, coaches, friends, Tina and her family, all save one—Ms. Jones. She no longer was my number one fan, and I still could not understand her change in heart toward me. She did vindictive things to me, including kicking me out of her home the night before my second ACT testing.

June 7, 2003, I earned my high school diploma. I was so proud of myself. I had accomplished one of my goals, to be a high school graduate. My next goal was to attend college and graduate. Goals kept me on track to better my life.

Sadly, though, the past can taint the joy of reaching a goal. The day of my high school graduation, the day marking my passage from boy to man, the day I should have been all smiles, my mother phoned me from hospital, stating that she could not attend my graduation because she was recovering from another of my father's beatings. Their sad lives had not changed a bit during my absence. Had I remained with them much longer, I am sure they would have steadily dragged me down to their level.

I sometimes wonder where I might be today, had the court not removed me from their self-destructive influences. Would I be a high school graduate or would I have dropped out? Would I have succumbed to alcohol, drugs and violence or gone on to college, married a loving woman and embraced the religious life? Only God can answer those questions. I forgive them, though. Jesus teaches us that forgiveness cleanses the soul and voids the past. Dwelling on the past is futile and self-defeating. The future is what matters.

By the end of my first year of college, my relationship with Ms. Jones came to an abrupt and eye-opening end. When my social worker quit sending funds to Ms. Jones for my support, diverting them to me at college, I learned the sad truth about our relationship. In front of my independent living worker, she stated I could "no longer live with her if the State would not pay for my bed." I had mistakenly believed that she loved me as a mother loves her son, rather than as a foster parent paid to care for a foster child. The fact that she concerned herself more about the money than she did about me nearly broke my heart.

By this time, though, I refused to let anybody or anything stop me from becoming somebody. I no longer blamed myself for the mistakes of my parents. I was through feeling sorry for myself and allowing other people to drag me down. I joined social organizations, such as the church gospel choir and various child advocacy groups, and majored in social work at college. My senior year in college I worked at a social services agency, gaining valuable experience in child welfare. I then combined my childhood experience with my education and professional expertise to work on behalf of other children who become clients of the foster care system.

Today, I work with the Annie E. Casey Foundation as a Technical Assistant. I travel throughout the United States assisting child welfare agencies that have the foresight to engage foster children in the process of improving the foster care system. My responsibility is to raise awareness of the needs of foster children and to promote systemic changes that improve the delivery of services to children in out-of-home care, such as securing them medical assistance and college scholarships. I am also happily married to my college girlfriend, LyAshia, and I am a college graduate, ordained minister and child advocate. I could not be happier! My life has come full circle.

As an alumnus of the system, I often use my childhood experiences to motivate current foster kids. They are so hungry for role models who give them hope for a brighter future. Abuse, neglect, violence, abandonment and other painful experiences have a way of eroding self-confidence and stifling the belief that someday "things will get better." Too many foster children give up while they are still in the system, and many more fail to adapt when they transition to the "real world." The pain of the past haunts them with negative feelings of being alone, disconnected, unlovable, worthless and doomed to a life of unrelenting angst. These dark feelings redouble at age 18, when an insensitive foster care system dumps them onto the streets without benefit of continued support and guidance. For too many ill-prepared foster children, emancipation leads to homelessness, substance abuse, prostitution, crime, imprisonment and other negative outcomes, a kind of "self-fulfilling prophecy" that these vulnerable young people often expect. I am one of the lucky ones, and I strive to use my life as an example for current foster children to better their lives.

I also encourage foster parents, caseworkers, group home staff, program administrators, policy-makers and government officials to re-double their efforts to safeguard the physical and mental health of foster children throughout their placement and to provide supportive services after emancipation. The transition to adult status is difficult for most children, and especially so for young people who lack family ties. If the childcare system indeed is the "surrogate parent" of foster children, the government must develop new and innovative programs, policies and procedures designed to enhance the potential for kids in out-of-home placement to mature into self-reliant adults, as would any caring biological parent.

Too many of my foster brothers and sisters are lost along the way to adulthood, sad statistics of an insensitive and inept system that has failed foster kids for generations. Perhaps it is time for the decision-makers to listen to those of us who have survived the system and utilize our input to fix what has too long been broken. Foster children need more than good intentions, lip service, food and shelter. We deserve a chance to grow beyond the darkness of the past to embrace a brighter future. By including the voices and insights of survivors, like those presented in this book, in the decision-making process, the child welfare system might just advance its mission of helping young people grow past difficult situations by learning from those of us who have surmounted seemingly impossible odds.

Surviving the Storm Inside Me: Growing Past Foster Care

Debraha Watson

Before I tell my story, it is important to relate my mother's beginnings, in part, because her family history and life circumstances most likely affected her mental health and her parenting ability. My mother, Nannie Geraldine Cox, was born January 27, 1933 in Williamson, West Virginia—a coal camp. Her mother died a few days after her birth on February 1, 1933. Following the funeral, her father bundled up his newborn and left her with his wife's best friend, Katie Parks, who was married but childless.

Katie Parks eventually took in my mother's two older sisters, Ruby and Juanita, and reared them until they came of age. My mother lived in the Parks' home until her thirteenth year, at which time she became pregnant. Stating that she was a religious woman and would not abide with my mother's ungodly behavior, Mrs. Parks asked my mother to leave her home. It is not known where she lived during this time, but rumor has it that she lived in the mountains until she went into labor. Alone and afraid, she returned to the coal camp, gave birth and was given a cup of broth and put back onto the streets. Katie Parks kept the child, my older sister Lois, and later adopted her. Nannie, preferring to use the name Geraldine, migrated to Michigan as a domestic, where she gained employment with an affluent family in Detroit. The family discharged her shortly after arriving because she demonstrated "strange behavior."

My mother's short life was troubled. She spent much of it in and out of mental health institutions, where she received the diagnosis of "reactionary schizophrenic." This may have accounted for her leaving my younger brother and me for days at a time with only bread and water. I also missed numerous days of school, which resulted in my having to repeat the third grade. The tenants of the hotel where we lived were dangerous and I saw and heard things a seven-year-old should neither see nor hear. It was also during this time when one of my mother's "friends" sexually abused me.

My brother and I came into the child welfare system April 20, 1960, following the death of my mother from childbirth complications. The child—a boy—died two days later. The social service records indicate that at the time, they could not locate any relatives and listed our father as "unknown." My brother Sandy and I went to live at the D.J. Healy Home for Wayward Children. I was seven and he was four at the time of placement. We remained at D.J. Healy until June 30, 1960. Following a court hearing that made us temporary wards of the court, the Children's Aid Society was ordered by the court to develop an adoption plan. Later the court retained permanent custody and we both became eligible for adoption without the customary six-month waiting period.

The court further investigated our case and determined that both my mothers' parents were deceased and her two living sisters indicated they did not want the children. We then entered our first foster home placement on the east side of Detroit.

Although I have read and re-read the records repeatedly, I do not remember much about my first foster home. Sandy and I were together for the first three foster home placements. From the case reports I learned that I was considered a very "grown-up child." In my first home, I adjusted well, with "few behavioral problems." I remained "protective and domineering over my younger brother." The troubling aspect appeared to be that I preferred the company of adults. After being in my first home for approximately six months, a progress report read:

"This child seems to be showing good progress towards adjusting to her situation and her social environment. She is a courteous and weak child. She can be submissive in her attitude towards others. Although it is felt that she is opinionated and will express herself if the situation presents so. She is reserved for her age, needs stimulation, encouragement and praise. She does not speak of her birth mother as she did when she was committed to care but it is felt that she still thinks a great deal of her natural family."

According to the records, I did well in school, receiving all Bs. My brother also fared well in this home. However, a year later, according to the reports, the boarding mother:

" . . . expressed openly her dislike for Debraha and her dislike or jealousy on the part of Debraha and the Boarding Father's relationship."

She also stated that she, the foster mother, when referring to my brother:

" . . . consistently complains of how lazy the child is and how unresponsive he is in caring for himself and learning the few tasks she asks of him."

In June of 1961, Sandy and I moved to another foster home, also located in East Detroit. I have vivid memories of this foster home, and find myself puzzled by the social worker's progress report stating that we transitioned well. I hated this home from the moment I set foot in it. I remember it being a big house, with big furniture, and there were starched white dollies everywhere. "Mother Rose," as we were to call her, even wore one on her head on Sundays when she went to church. Mother Rose was a big-bosomed, heavy-armed, sun-bleached yellow-skinned woman with beautiful hair. It was long and thick, worn tightly coiled around her head in one long braid. Her eyes seemed too small for a woman her size. They were almost slits that upturned slightly at the corners. She had thin lips with a moustache almost as heavy as that of her husband's. I privately called her "snake woman," although I no longer remember why. I can only remember her wearing a white uniform and walking on the back of Mr. Anderson's worn leather house shoes. The shoes were much too big for her and often—too often—I dreamt of shuffling footsteps on the polished black and white linoleum. Then I would startle awake having pulled all of the sheets off the bed.

In contrast to Mother Rose, I remember little about Mr. Anderson. He was a tall, wiry man, who always wore work clothes: dull grey overalls, flannel shirts and heavy black work boots covered with mud, which he tracked into the house. He always carried a metal lunch box and smelled of motor oil. Unlike Mother Rose, he was quiet. To be honest, I do not remember his ever saying much to any of us. He was just there, like another big fixture in the house. Perhaps like us, he was afraid to do anything but breathe . . . quietly.

I learned to work in this house. We polished furniture, silver and the winding oak banister that led upstairs. I scrubbed floors on my hands and knees, as Mother Rose didn't believe in mops. This was a sparkling clean house with everything in place. The only chore that we escaped was washing and ironing, though we had the responsibility of hanging out the laundry on the clothesline in the summer. I was also the only one with kitchen duty. I made breakfast, usually oatmeal or corn meal mush, rind bacon and oven toast. I also shelled peas, picked greens and helped with canning vegetables and making jelly in preparation for the long harsh winters. I remember dragging cast iron skillets out of the pantry, which were much too heavy for me to lift, and her yelling at me for scarring up her shiny-waxed floors, when I dropped them.

There was another child in the home, a girl about my age. Her name was Rosalyn - a frail child, who always fidgeted. She twirled her long black braids around her fingers as she sucked her thumb. Mother Rose coated her thumb with all types of disgusting things to keep her from putting it in her mouth. She told her she was ugly enough without having bucked teeth, and warned that her thumb was going to fall off eventually. I wanted to befriend Rosalyn but we did not play together much because she was so quiet and scared of everything. While I remember the house and its contents, I do not recall having any friends in this home, although the case records show that I attended Hillger Elementary School, was in grade four, received average grades and had average conduct. The records also noted that I was an alert and conscientious student, and stated that I loved to read "a great deal about animals."

It was in this foster home that I developed a habit of stealing and lying, which resulted in Mother Rose threatening us with beatings. Mother Rose kept money hidden under those starched dollies, and I began sneaking a dollar here and there to buy penny candy to make friends. My friends only lasted as long as I had candy.

Mother Rose was a deeply religious woman, although I cannot remember the church we attended. She read us scriptures and spoke often of the importance of being good. Based on her practice of whipping us each night before we went to bed for a sin she knew we had committed but perhaps did not see, I came to believe that if I were going to get beaten anyway I might as well steal.

During these whippings, I refused to cry. I bit the inside of my lips, my tongue, anything to keep from crying out. I stiffened my body against the lashes and stood there defiantly. Mother Rose hit me harder, determined to break me, but I tired her out and often she had little remaining energy to beat Sandy and Rosalyn. Many times, they escaped the physical punishment, although I will never forget the fear in their eyes.

When my beating was over, she would tell me, "say your prayers and go to bed." After the lights went out, I cried silently in the dark. Not surprisingly, I experienced a worsening of my asthmatic condition, receiving treatment several times at Children's Hospital. Asthma can be triggered when those affected are subjected to emotional or psychological stress and I was a child with a storm raging inside me.

Eventually, the abuse became unbearable and I tried to kill myself by swallowing baby aspirin and eating a box of Ex-Lax. I was very ill and I got a terrible beating for going into the medicine cabinet.

The case reports do not say why the court removed Sandy from this home first, although they do document that he was "lazy and maladjusted." My records indicate that I did not adjust well to our separation. In fact, I ran away after school. I walked for hours reading street signs and dodging adults. As night fell, I was bone cold and had to use the bathroom. I wandered into someone's garage to relieve myself.

I tried sleeping in the garage but the cement was too cold and hard. I also heard strange noises and became scared, so I wandered on. Not knowing where else to go, I returned to the school playground, where I tried to sleep inside a cement tunnel balled up in the fetal position with my coat tightly wrapped about me, but the ground was cold and lumpy. I slept for a while, but the night air woke me up, and in defeat, I walked back to Mother Rose's house. I planned to sleep on the porch, get up before daylight and try again. Mr. Anderson thwarted my plans when he heard a noise and turned on the porch light.

The police and social worker came and questioned me. Where had I been? Why did I run away? Did anybody mess with me down there? I do not remember what time it was, although it was still dark when they took me from the home. My clothes were already packed. The social worker, accompanied by the police, took me to a hospital, where I underwent psychological testing. In June of 1962, I went to another foster home where Sandy and I lived together again, and for a while, I was happy.

The Whitings were transplanted Mississippians who were childless until Sandy and I arrived in the home. The Whiting household was a sharp contrast to the Anderson's home. Their home was "lived in," meaning it was not nasty but it was not as clean and tidy as Mother Rose's house. Mrs. Whiting kept her precious French provincial living room furniture covered with plastic, but she wasn't fussy about dust or fingerprints.

Mrs. Whiting was a fun loving woman who taught me to cook and play baseball. I loved Mrs. Whiting, but I feared her husband, even though now I can't remember him doing anything to me that should have caused those feelings. Perhaps it is because I had seen her cower under his verbal wrath. If dinner weren't on the table at a certain time . . . if we made too much noise playing . . . if we broke one of his many rules . . . if anything were out of order in the house, we heard about it. One of his rules was when Big Time wrestling came on television everything and everybody, including our dog Bullet, a German Shepherd, had to be still and quiet.

I credit Miss Clarice Nancarrow, the Principal of Nichols Elementary school, for giving me the attention I sorely needed to excel in school. She would ask me what I had read that week and provided me copies of the *Weekly Reader*. We read poetry and talked about the adventures of Nancy Drew and the Hardy Boys. She tactfully taught me about hygiene and the importance of a young lady "keeping her appearance." When she found out I had few clothes, most of which were threadbare and oversized, she brought in dresses from a relative to wear for special occasions, such as school assemblies and plays.

I learned to love school. I excelled in every subject, except math. I had few friends and preferred to lose myself in books. Books allowed me to have an identity. I could place myself in the scene and become anyone I wanted to be. Without a book in my possession, I had to become invisible and not draw attention to myself. I read everything I could get my hands on. I often handled my painful and unsafe world by withdrawing into fantasy. I would read and integrate images of colorful characters with places found in the discarded worn pages of *National Geographic* magazines that Mr. Whiting brought home. Sitting in one place, I could take myself across the world.

As much as I tried to keep a low profile at school there were bullies that sought me out and teased or beat me up after school. They made up rhymes about my being left in the garbage and not knowing the identity of my parents. They also called me names because I wore hand-me-downs or ill-fitting clothes. Mr. Whiting - having been an amateur boxer before he left Mississippi - taught me how to throw a punch and duck to avoid punches. I became a sixth grade gladiator.

The years in the Whiting household came and went. It was in the summer of 1965, my third year there, when my life began to unravel and things changed at home. Although I cannot remember the sequence of events, several things happened. I was still stealing and got caught. My foster mother's brother started making inappropriate advances and exposing himself to me, and I began running with a neighborhood gang of "hoodlums." The gang gave me a sense of belonging, and although we did nothing dangerous, we destroyed property, stole from the neighborhood store and drank homemade wine. My stint in the gang was short lived. We dispersed after the summer as we entered junior high school.

That fall I entered seventh grade at Butzel Junior High School. This was a new world for me and, of course, I did not fit in. I had a bad case of acne on my forehead, thick unruly hair that refused to stay in place and my clothes never fit, as I was especially frail. The Children's Aid Society based clothing orders on a sizing chart for what a child of a certain age "should" wear. Mrs. Whiting always ordered our shoes too large so that we could "grow into them." I stuffed the toes with paper to keep them from sliding off as I walked. Everywhere I went, such as the cafeteria, the library and class, students were in cliques and I thought they were talking about me: that ugly bumpy faced, nappy-headed girl. I was the outsider and I didn't know how to make friends. Instead, I would stand around sulking, watching and listening to other students' conversations. I was at that school for half a semester before my life changed once again.

Leaving the Whiting household took me by surprise. I thought I would stay there forever, that they would adopt Sandy and me and we would live happily ever after. I had gained a degree of acceptance at school and counted a few neighborhood kids as friends. The emotional climate in the household did not register in my twelve-year-old mind.

Things were unremarkable at school the day I left the Whiting household. Before the dismissal bell rang, I heard my name over the intercom. My heart dropped, because I knew a call to the Principal's Office meant one thing: I was in trouble. Weak-kneed and trembling, I slowly made my way to the main office, my mind questioning: What have I done now? When I arrived in the Principal's Office, there sat Miss Jones, the social worker. She said in a matter of fact tone, "Get your coat and belongings." I did as she instructed, walking out of the school building, into the cold crisp February air and into her lime green Ford station wagon. I recognized my raggedy suitcase with the broken latch lying on the back seat of the car, tied closed with one of Mr. Whiting's belts. This same suitcase held our belongings after our mother died. Stuffed brown paper bags held the rest of my clothing. Miss Jones told me not to cry. I sat on my knees looking out of the back window of the Ford wagon as we drove off, crying and planning my escape.

Miss Jones informed me that I was moving to a new home. I asked her a flurry of questions. Why was I moving? Did I do something wrong? Where was I going? Where was Sandy? Was I going to see Mr. and Mrs. Whiting before I left? She never answered; instead, she lectured me on sex and the importance of being a "good girl." She also warned me that if I did not behave at this home, the court would most likely place me in juvenile detention until I became of age. I sat silently, a human inferno, looking out the window, attempting to memorize street signs, landmarks, anything that would help me find my way "home." Finally, realizing that we had been driving for a long time, I asked where I was going. She told me my new home was in Inkster, Michigan, which might as well have been the planet Mars to me.

My final foster home was located thirty miles outside the city of Detroit. My foster parents had a daughter four years older than I was. She hated me on sight and I had made up my mind to hate them. I refused to speak to anyone in the household and my form of communication was grunts, nodding yes and no or hunching my shoulders. I went to bed every night thinking about Sandy. I was angry with him because he got a chance to stay with the Whitings.

Starting another new school was just as difficult as joining another new foster family. I knew from my previous moves what to expect from school. The new kid always caught hell. I quickly learned that telling kids from rural Inkster that I was from the east side of Detroit automatically meant I was tough. Few of my classmates challenged me.

Shortly after I came to this home, other foster girls began arriving. Some stayed a few weeks, others several months. I eventually learned to treat them like guests. I have forgotten most of their names and faces, after all these years. They would be there for just a short while, and then return to their families. I felt that I had no one, that I was all alone, a worthless child with no family, not even a brother . . . anymore. I resigned myself to the fact that I would remain there until I turned eighteen.

I continued to do well in school and eventually gained a few friends. The memories of my brother Sandy also started to fade and I figured he would be lost to me forever. Eventually I came out of my shell and began integrating into the family as much as could be allowed. I was always the "foster child" who was reminded that I should be grateful these people opened their home to me. I showed my gratitude by being an overachiever at everything to make them proud. The Holdsclaws, however, did not give praise or rewards.

The foster care records dated October 17, 1969 noted:

"Debraha is very anxious to know a little about her family. She wonders where the natural mother was buried and if she really has a sister named Lois Marie. Debraha states that the social worker told her that she does not have a sister, but she believes she has."

My inquisitiveness started an investigation, and the Children's Aid Society found that I did indeed have a sister raised in West Virginia. At the time of my high school graduation in 1971, I briefly reunited with my sister Lois, who was married with two children, and my brother Sandy, who had gone through three more foster homes. Shortly thereafter, he entered a juvenile facility, and then prison.

When I graduated, like many other alumni, I had no transition plan. I assumed I would get a job but even then, with limited skills, I could not find employment to support myself. I lived with friends, in bus stations and transitional housing, namely the YWCA and Evangeline Residence for Women.

After spending two years in limbo, I finally reached a point where I thought I had more stability. Quite by accident, I ran into a childhood friend looking for a roommate. She invited me to share her apartment; shortly thereafter, I found a full time job at a finance company. Life was good . . . at least for a little while. After working for a few months, I became involved with another employee and found myself pregnant. When I informed him of my condition, he was non-supportive. At the same time, my roommate announced her engagement and asked me to move as soon as possible. Scared and desperate, I asked my former foster mother if I could return to her home until I found another place to live. She reluctantly agreed, yet reminded me daily of my condition and shame.

I felt I had nowhere to turn. I was not close to my sister in West Virginia at that time and had lost track of my brother, who had entered the penal system. To escape my foster mother's verbal tirades, I spent much of my time at the local community center, eventually befriending the older brother of a former classmate. He immediately took an interest in me. After only two dates, he proposed and, out of desperation, I said "yes." I married—primarily to have a home in which to live and to feel a sense of belonging.

The hasty and loveless marriage was short-lived and marred by abuse. Unable to support my infant son, I found myself on the welfare rolls. Determined not to be dependent upon the system again, I entered community college and after three years gained employment as a Respiratory Therapist. I eventually continued my education through graduate school, completing my Ph.D. in 2001.

My foster care experiences affected me in numerous ways. Perhaps most of all, I never had the opportunity to reconnect emotionally with my younger brother Sandy. I was so busy trying to stay alive that I devoted little time to keeping in touch with him. He became lost in the prison system, addicted to heroin, and then crack. Upon his release from prison, he visited me once and we talked perhaps three times over the next five years. He died of AIDS, leaving me a shoebox full of cassette tapes he had recorded chronicling his short life to the backdrop of the blues music of Miles Davis. Foster care killed him a little bit at a time, tormenting his soul and robbing him of an identity, reducing him to an addict who escaped the reality of his loveless, transient life through drug-induced stupor. I still grieve for him daily. His death brought my sister Lois and me closer, although having been adopted at birth, I am sure she does not and cannot understand my trials in foster care, or those suffered by our deceased brother.

Like so many other foster children, I carry scars from growing up without a sense of family, security and permanency to ground me emotionally and psychologically. I still have trust issues and I am over-protective of my children. I can be abrupt and more than a few people have told me that I do not have much of a sense of humor. Conversely, though, I have strong survival skills and I handle stress and change better than most people do.

People often ask me how I survived my experiences and, unfortunately, I do not have any great words of wisdom, and I am cautious about giving advice. I use my life experiences and education to teach foster care professionals how to help their clients through difficult times and teach foster and delinquent children how to become self-sufficient and how to put a difficult past behind them.

I wish there were easy solutions to the debacle that is the foster care system, but there are not any. How can a system of care undo the emotional damage done by mothers and fathers who abused, neglected or abandoned their own children? Still, it is individuals within the system, not the flawed system itself, who can make a difference in what foster children experience in out-of-home care. It is these "dedicated foster care workers" to whom I now speak. You CAN and often DO make a positive difference in our foster care experiences and adult outcomes.

Keeping siblings together must be a priority. It is paramount that foster children retain some sense of familial identity. It is difficult enough for us to deal with removal from our parents or other adult family members, but by also separating us from our brothers and sisters, we now are stripped of all sense of family—cut adrift, alone and unconnected to anything or anyone. If this is not possible, develop ways for us to stay in touch and, at minimum, maintain accurate records regarding the siblings' placements so that we can find one another in the future.

Screen foster families carefully, monitor them closely and train them well. Too many vulnerable foster children suffer physical, emotional and sexual abuse, neglect and even death at the hands of those charged with protecting us. Maltreatment by caregivers damages our emotional stability, creating trust issues and other psychological problems that fester deep inside, negatively affecting our behaviors and outlook on life, often . . . too often . . . translating into adjustment problems that handicap our potential to adapt and succeed in childhood and beyond. Monitor our progress carefully, being sensitive to sudden or dramatic changes that may symbolize our unsophisticated "cry for help." Advocate on our behalf and safeguard us as you would your own children and we will flourish. Fail to do so, and as surely as day becomes night, we will suffer the consequences both during and after we leave the system.

Multiple placements damage us, often beyond repair. Stability is essential to our wellbeing. Every time a foster child moves from one placement to another, he or she feels that much more abandoned, rejected and worthless. Imagine believing each move symbolizes that nobody wants you, and that each new placement emphasizes your separation from the rest of society. Adjusting to new people, new rules, new surroundings, new everything, promotes adjustment problems, ultimately leading to other behavioral and emotional problems. Is it any wonder, then, that so many of us fail to transition successfully to a world we have come to believe has no place for us?

There must be a holistic approach to developing transitional plans for youth aging out of the system. Dumping us onto the streets at eighteen without support and guidance further emphasizes our lack of value, and hamstrings our future. Loving parents know that the transition from dependent child to independent adult does not always go smoothly and therefore they understand the importance of continued support throughout this difficult maturation process. Sadly, foster children must learn to sink or swim on their own, without benefit of a lifeline. There is no doubt that this obvious lack of continued support during this difficult transitional period lays waste to too many of us, who end up on the streets homeless, pregnant, drug addicted, diseased and destined for a life of problems, including early death and imprisonment. This lack of responsibility—of "humaneness"—by a heartless system must undergo a dramatic metamorphosis.

The foster care system will not change by itself; rather, it is incumbent upon the caring and dedicated professionals working within the system to change it, so that foster children can know a better life. I count on you, dear reader: be a catalyst for change, for without you, the system has no heart or soul, merely perpetuating itself, ruining too many more of us with its arcane and insensitive programs, policies and procedures. We deserve better treatment— much better!

Upward Bound In Foster Care:
What Worked For Me
and What Remains To Be Done

❦

Meloney Barney

While many children inherit family privilege, heirlooms and other assets from their parents and grandparents, my legacy condemned me to a life as a ward of the state. My great-grandmother passed the torch of childrearing failure to her daughter, and she, in turn, handed it down to her daughter, who, in sequence, would have passed it on to me. Fortunately, however, it has been my good fortune to break this seemingly perpetual cycle of family dysfunction. Aside from divine intervention, I must credit nonconformity for the success of this blatantly rebellious act.

Being a foster child was, for me, hell on earth. My transition from living with a dysfunctional mother and stepfather to residing in a foster care placement with a witch of a guardian truly deprived me of knowing genuine happiness in my youth. Recalling the dire series of events that led to the division of my family never completely leaves my mind, almost as if they took place yesterday. In fact, I am still healing. Although I pray that I will not repeat the traumatic episodes I experienced so early in my life, I have forgiven those responsible, though, sadly, I am unable to forget, which is why I doubt I will make the same mistakes. Indeed, I strive to make sure that my adult life in no way approximates the ensuing story of my childhood.

Perhaps the best place to begin is when our family of seven lived in the Metro Lodge. My four siblings and I attended school during the week, followed by two after-school programs before returning to the motel where my mother worked to provide us shelter. It was supposed to be a temporary arrangement, something to get us through the current predicament into which my stepfather managed to put us.

My mother lived in fear of losing custody of us. Her mother lost custody of her as a child and the idea of it happening to her own offspring weighed heavily on her mind. I still hear her reassuring me that things would get better, just before she apologized for the way things really were. "Meloney, honey, the good life is just around the corner," she forced a smile and lightly touched my cheek, "I'm so very sorry for putting you through all of this," she then whispered, and turned her face, as if to hide her shame.

Although I had a grasp of our precarious situation, along with the litany of bad decisions leading up to our poor living conditions, I never once held her accountable. Even if we had to live on the streets, as long as she and I stayed together, she remained innocent in my eyes. My stepfather, on the other hand, was the culprit I blamed for taking her down the path to destruction.

Before he came along, there were just the two of us, my mother and me. She worked at an airport, while I attended elementary school not far from the new home into which we had just moved, after relocating from Michigan to Ohio. I was much too young to understand what loneliness meant to an adult, and by the time I did discover its importance, it was too late. By then, my stepfather had married my mother and she had given birth to my three half-brothers and one half-sister, sealing our fate.

To this day, I cannot fathom why my mother got involved with my stepfather or why she remained with him, given his dependence on drugs and his explosive temper. He was either high on crack, cocaine, heroin, meth or some other mind-numbing substance or busy bullying my mother or me. He certainly did not deserve my mother's love, but she gave it to him nonetheless. I can only guess that she was either too desperate for the love of a man or too scared to leave him. Whatever her reason, I was subjected to many uncomfortable situations, some with, and others without, her knowledge.

Oh, how I hated that man. His constant substance and domestic abuse sapped the life from my mother and ruined my childhood. He never once abused my siblings, though, I assume because they were blood. My mother and I, however, did not share his lineage and proved perfect scapegoats for his drug-addled rages. I lived in constant fear that one day he would kill us.

I have to give my mother high marks for finding the courage to finally take us away from my stepfather and go into hiding. We left with just the clothes on our backs, living on the cold, late-fall streets of Cleveland, while a church supplied us with food. The caseworker from a homeless shelter referred my mother to a domestic abuse shelter, where we were fortunate to reside until my mother got back on her feet. It was truly by the grace of God that she found the strength to fight past her own addictions and regain enough stability to relocate us to another state and start anew.

We moved into a home of our own in Detroit, Michigan. My siblings and I enrolled in school or daycare. Mom sought work, but received public assistance during the interim. Our lives began turning around. What mattered most, though, was being stable and far away from my stepfather. It felt so good to enjoy peace of mind without fearing for our lives. However, the solitude lasted only briefly, two months to be exact. After my mother made a few ill-advised telephone calls to family members, someone told my stepfather where we lived and he appeared one day, unannounced, uninvited and repentant. Much to my dismay, my mother accepted him back into our lives and the cycle began again.

My stepfather somehow convinced my mother that he had changed his ways; he claimed to have "conquered the demons" of his drug dependence and his anger problems. Hallelujah! It was a miracle. He almost had us believing him too, until a few weeks later, when some very dangerous men broke into our home to collect his drug debt. After nearly beating him to death, my stepfather escaped out the bedroom window and made it to a hospital for treatment, leaving us alone with the enraged men. My mother felt compelled to take action for the safety of her five children and the unconditional love she felt for my stepfather. In an effort to spare all our lives, she offered our house as a transaction center for the drug dealers to conduct their business.

Having drug dealers posted in our home around the clock turned us into prisoners. Even though they forgave my stepfather's drug debt, our home life suffered horribly. Not only was it embarrassing for neighbors to classify our home a "crack house," but they also would not allow their children to play with us. Furthermore, I missed an entire year of school to stay home and take care of my four siblings. My mother no longer could handle the responsibility on her own, because of her own drug dependency. I did the grocery shopping, cooking, cleaning and care-giving for my half-brothers and sisters, who were still very young. My stepfather's return forced me to sacrifice my youth.

That was not all my stepfather took from me. He stole my innocence, too, or, more accurately, he traded my virtue to satisfy his addiction. He allowed the drug dealers to abuse me sexually in lieu of payment for his drugs. They sneaked into my attic bedroom in the dead of night to touch and fondle me. Then one of them went the whole way, threatening to kill my three-year-old baby sister if I did not cooperate. A second drug dealer orally molested me and forced me to do likewise to him. Despite feeling terrible shame and disgust, I never said a word to my mother, but my stepfather knew. To him, I was no more than a bartering chip in a drug transaction, a way to get his drugs free or on the cheap. How could he allow them to do such vile things to me? Why did he not love and protect me? Was I of less value than a rock of his beloved crack? I was only ten-and-a-half-years-old!

After 18 months imprisoned in the crack house, the police raided our home. Thankfully, we were not present for the intense home invasion, which included a smashed front door, broken windows and a living room that looked as if a tornado had blown through it. My stepfather had pulled yet another of his dumb stunts with the drug dealers and owed them a large sum of money; so much money, in fact, that my mother could not have negotiated anything remotely suitable to satisfy his enormous debt. In a desperate attempt to save himself from the wrath of the drug dealers, my stepfather had turned police informant and helped them to coordinate the raid. Before I knew what was happening, my stepfather hauled us out of our home to the Metro Lodge.

Motel residents began monitoring our presence the moment we moved in. In less than a month, someone called the authorities, reporting that our living condition was unsuitable for children. The Metro Lodge was a run-down place of last resort for society's rejects: the homeless, welfare recipients, mental patients, parolees, prostitutes, drug addicts and drug dealers. Night had arrived and we children were preparing for bed, when a State of Michigan social worker, accompanied by uniformed police, arrived to remove us from the premises. That was the last time we would live together as a family. It was the saddest day of my life, the day I became a ward of the state.

I cried, shook, squirmed, begged and pleaded for my mommy while the social worker questioned me and filled out paperwork. I had no clue why we five children had been hustled away from our parents. Did we do something wrong? Was it because of the drug dealers at our house? Had my stepfather sold us all out?

The Demby Memorial Children's Group Home looked like a college campus, with manicured lawns, ancient trees and rustic buildings. If memory serves me correctly, three cottages housed the children: a boys' cottage, a girls' cottage and a cottage for special-needs kids. What I remember most about my brief stay at Demby was that I could not stop crying the entire time I stayed there, so deeply had the trauma of separation from my mother affected me.

My baby sister, Melissa, who lived with me at the girls' cottage, however, never shed a tear or displayed any emotions. In fact, she had yet to utter her first word, despite nearing her fourth birthday. That is probably when I first noticed she had something wrong with her, although I could neither understand nor articulate it at the time. With the advantage of hindsight, though, I now realize that when my mother joined my stepfather in abusing drugs, she continued to do so throughout her pregnancies, thereby affecting all four of their offspring. To this day, I wonder about her lifestyle when I was in her womb.

Sixteen days after placement at Demby, an elderly couple named Taylor took an interest in Melissa and me. Melissa and I stayed in the elderly couple's home until Mrs. Taylor learned that Melissa was autistic and had her returned to Demby. Melissa and my three half-brothers, Adrian, Andre and Anthony moved three times, before a family from Albuquerque, New Mexico adopted them. A foster family that specialized in special-needs foster children eventually adopted Melissa.

Still grieving over the loss of my family, losing Melissa took me over the edge. With no remaining connection to my family, I felt totally abandoned, unwanted, lost, confused, frightened, alone . . . so terribly alone. Like an emotional pinball machine, I went on tilt. Nothing in my life made sense. I began to see myself as truly worthless and unlovable. Perhaps my stepfather was right about me all along. I was of less value than a rock of crack. I did not deserve to live. I hated myself, worthless little girl that I was.

That is when thoughts of suicide began short-circuiting my brain. I would just end it all, this miserable life that only got worse and worse, like crap circling down a toilet bowl. I was truly ready to die. I failed in my first two suicide attempts, using pills and choking devices that only produced fainting and nausea. If I had not met just the right person at this pivotal moment in my life, I am sure that I would have succeeded in killing myself the third time or at least harmed myself seriously, so severe was my emotional confusion, self-hatred and gut need to die. I just needed to stop the pain. I was going to kill myself, and that was that. I very likely might have, had I not met Dr. Rosalind Folman, a researcher who asked to interview me about my foster care experiences and academic progress. I connected to her in a way that I could not establish with any of the social workers I had during my foster care journey. They treated me like a job, not a person, and they always took sides with the caregivers, not with me. I will forever appreciate Dr. Folman for her genuine interest and concern for my well-being. She came into my life at just the right moment to save me from killing myself. Perhaps it was divine intervention.

When I learned that Dr. Folman had been a foster child, too, my defense mechanisms vanished. Here was somebody I instinctively knew would understand me, not judge me. I never felt the level of trust and comfort with the therapists, social workers, counselors and other foster care professionals that I did with Dr. Folman. She knew my pain. She understood me. She had lived a childhood similar to my own and grown past it. She helped me to understand that I did not have to end up like my mother. Dr. Folman helped me to believe that I was a unique and amazing person. She was the only adult who took an interest in me at a time when I needed it most. She became my role model, the wise and caring mother figure I so desperately yearned for and needed. The more interest Dr. Folman took in me, the more I found reason to keep living. She is the person who pulled me back from the brink of self-destruction and put me on the path to self-realization. It is only now that I am reflecting on my foster care experience that I realize how positively she affected my thought processes and actions. Because of her continued support and guidance, I also managed to survive placement with my foster parents, specifically Mrs. Taylor.

At first, the elderly couple seemed as if they had my best interests at heart. They were people of faith who lived a simple life and attended church functions several times per week. With the passing of time, however, I became increasingly aware that my foster mother constantly nagged, complained or accused my foster father. It was not long before I took over my foster father's role and became the new target for her verbal tirades and false accusations. She accused me of the most ridiculous and petty transgressions, such as holding the door open to let flies in the house, purposely failing to put the cap on the toothpaste container or deliberately dragging dirt into the house on the bottom of my shoes. She seemed to think that I was defiant and spiteful to her and that I did not show her anywhere near the respect she deserved for giving me a place to live.

False accusations were not the only negative issues I endured within her home. My foster mother was domineering, possessive and uncompromising. Because I felt so uncomfortable around her, I sought refuge by pursuing activities outside the house, such as volunteering at church and participating in after-school events. It felt good to be involved with other kids, to develop relationships and to share my thoughts and concerns with friends. Sadly, confiding in my foster mother always backfired. She twisted my words and took delight in making me look like a liar or a fool.

My first attempt to connect with my foster mother serves as an example. I confided in her about my misgivings with my biological mother's decision to permit the drug dealers to take over our home, to save her family from possible harm. My foster mother repeated this confidential information to her relatives who, by the time the story got back to me, described my biological mother as a "sleazy drug-addict" who intentionally put her children in harm's way. I refused to give credence to my foster mother's rendition of my story and reiterated what I had initially said, although I really did not want her family knowing my history. This attempt to set the record straight angered my foster mother, who threatened to send me back to Demby and grounded me for two weeks.

I could not risk returning to Demby, so I acquiesced to the validity of that story and everything else my foster mother said about my biological family or me. I carefully chose my words and watched my behavior so that I did not come off as defiant or disruptive. I walked on eggshells for years.

My foster mother often inquired about her husband's relationship with me. She even asked if he had molested me, based on her perverted assessment of how well he and I got along. My foster father never molested or harmed me in any way. He was a good man who loved and respected me a million times more than my stepfather had. He encouraged my educational goals and advised me on survival techniques to cope with living with my foster mother. He made living with her almost tolerable.

My physical health also presented issues for my foster mother. I will never forget when EMS had to transport me from school to the emergency unit for treatment of severe menstrual pains, where the doctors discovered I had a feminine reproductive problem known as "endometriosis." When the hospital called to report my condition, my foster mother was reluctant to come get me. She held a high position in the church, where she was attending a very important service when the hospital called to apprise her of my medical condition. She arrived four hours later, infuriated, demanding that the doctors release me immediately. According to her, women did not discuss their feminine issues and as far as she was concerned, hospitalization for intense cramping was absurd. She was in her seventies and I was barely fourteen at the time. She scolded me all the way home and accused me of being nothing more than a huge interruption in her life. Instead of sending me back to Demby, which she threatened to do constantly, she doubled my household chores and further restricted my nearly nonexistent social life.

Not only did she deprive me of interacting with peers outside of school, I could only talk on the phone when she was present to monitor the conversation. I never attended slumber parties, and, although I could have visitors, we had to remain on the front porch and sit on the same level. If I ventured off the porch or sat lower or higher than my guests did, they had to leave and I remained housebound the rest of the evening. I spent much of my time either in the house or on the front porch, kind of like a criminal on house arrest, except I did not wear an ankle bracelet. Instead, my foster mother tethered me to an invisible leash that stretched only to the bottom step of her house, where I sat watching the other neighbor kids at play, unable to join in.

What hurt the most was her refusal to refer to me as her daughter or even as a member of her family. Instead, she called me her "foster child" and made it a point to tell me countless times how she did not feel that I was "one of her own." It did not matter what I tried to do to win her affection or approval, she would never regard me as family. I was the spawn of a sleazy drug-addict, a pedigree beneath her standards. It did not even matter how many accolades I achieved at school and church, I would always just be her "foster child." Once I finally accepted my fate within her home, I focused my energy and redirected my stress into my education. I vowed that her insensitive put downs would not reduce me to what my former foster care worker once told me. She said, "Most foster girls either fail out of school or get pregnant and end up on the streets." Fearing that I might repeat the mistakes made by my biological mother, her mother and the thousands of foster girls alluded to by my former foster care worker, I made a commitment to avoid becoming another negative foster care statistic.

After years of emotional abuse, a series of events made it possible for me to leave my placement with the Taylors and live with a friend's family my senior year of high school. At the beginning of the school year, my foster mother and I were embroiled in another of our ugly disagreements, when she threatened to have me removed from her home. Much to her surprise, and mine, this time I did not back down. I had had enough of her making me feel emotionally insecure, burdensome and unworthy. Not only did I call her bluff, I phoned my social worker and begged her to remove me, despite the possible consequences. She placed me in the foster home of the Walton family.

Perhaps the animosity I felt for Mrs. Taylor spilled over on the Walton family, because within a few weeks, I ran away from this placement and my social worker felt that I should reside in a treatment foster home until she could devise a better plan. During the interim, I continued to attend the same high school I had when living with the Taylor family, although I now had to catch three city buses to get there. Despite the long commute, I was always on time and my grades remained stellar. That is when my best friend MeShawn asked her mother if I could reside with their family. Imagine my surprise when both her mother and my social worker agreed to the idea. Thanks to my friend and her family, I finally found a place where I experienced love and stability, a home in which I felt like a valued family member.

Where in my former placements time seemingly stood dead still, my senior year of high school whizzed by in the nurturing care of the Freeman family. That spring, I began my "Student Independent Living" classes, consisting of two brief training sessions that did little to prepare me for emancipation. I wish now that the system would have taken the initiative to teach me more about how to transition from foster care to independent living. It would have helped me, as I am sure it would have helped many other foster children. Perhaps this lack of concern for what happens to us post-foster care is why my social worker forewarned me "most foster girls either fail out of school or get pregnant and end up on the streets." The system just does not adequately prepare us for adulthood, and, consequently, too many of us merely transition from the foster care system to another government system, such as the welfare system, criminal justice system or mental health system. Growing up is not easy; even less so when we must attempt to do it without the continued support and guidance of our parents or guardians.

Graduation quickly followed completion of Student Independent Living Classes. The years of redirecting my stress and focusing my energy into my education finally paid dividends. I achieved an overall grade point average of 3.9 and graduated Summa Cum Laude. Wayne State University even accepted me to pursue a degree in Biological Sciences. I was on my way to becoming a college student.

I cannot speculate what might have happened to me had I not been enabled to transition from the foster care system directly to the higher education system. I would like to think that I would not have ended up a client in one of the other government systems previously mentioned, as so many other foster kids do. College certainly did make emancipation easier for me. I had a goal of earning a college degree that kept me focused. Furthermore, I received financial aid from Wayne State University, as well as a Pepsi Grant, Pell Grant, federal student aid through FAFSA and a state funded studio apartment for much of my college career. Looking back on my time in foster care and post-foster care, education certainly provided the lifeline I needed to survive and thrive. Even now, I continue course work toward a master's degree in elementary education.

Neither can I know what might have happened to me had I remained with my drug-abusing mother and stepfather. I suspect, however, that my adult outcome would not have turned out as well as it has. Indeed, I probably would have carried on the family tradition of childrearing failure that has led generations of my female family members to repeat the mistakes of their predecessors. For helping me to break the cycle of family dysfunction, my husband, two children and I thank the foster care system.

Even today, at 30 years old, I still have issues to resolve, remnants of the past that cast dark shadows on my thoughts and behaviors. The worst of these issues involves my ability to love my husband unconditionally. Please, do not get me wrong; he is a wonderful, hardworking man, who treats me with loving tenderness. However, growing up without a biological father, then living with my self-centered, drug abusing stepfather and experiencing rape and perversion by the drug dealers has left deep scars that I pray some day will heal. Perhaps that is why I took my undergraduate degree in psychology, to understand how to help myself resolve this and other issues ingrained in my psyche at such an impressionable age. With the continued love and support of my wonderful husband, I think this too shall come to pass.

If I could have three wishes to improve the foster care system, based on my own experiences, wish number one would involve making sure all foster children routinely meet with a psychologist throughout their stay in the system and several years thereafter. Growing up in the care of strangers affects a child's mind, and the circumstances that led to removal from the family usually involves trauma. Similarly, the insecurity that results from multiple placements and living with foster parents not suited to raising foster children blunts their emotional growth. Burdened by years of unresolved issues and questions, we often leave the foster care system with psychological problems that limit our ability to mature emotionally. I suspect that is one reason why so many of us end up enmeshed in other government systems as adults, rather than successfully transitioning to independence.

Wish number two takes me back to when Dr. Folman saved me from my third suicide attempt. I had received some counseling while in placement, but it was sporadic and I never developed a rapport with the therapist. That is one reason why I did not answer her questions or provide insights that might have helped her to help me to resolve some of my issues. The other reason I did not respond to my therapist involved my perception of her as not being able to understand me. How could someone who obviously did not share my family and foster care background guide me, if they could not identify with my experiences? When I met Dr. Folman, however, who was a former foster child, not a therapist; I opened up like a flower at dawn. She was so like me. She so understood me. She knew my pain and confusion. She sensed my thoughts, often finishing my sentences for me. She was the wise confidant whose advice I followed as though it came from the Bible. Not even Sigmund Freud could have counseled me better, so imperative was it for me to receive the benefit of relating to someone who had walked in my shoes. I know I am not the only foster kid who feels this way. We need to bring more former foster children back into the system as foster care professionals, to provide current foster children with role models, mentors and confidants who can use their experiences to ease the way for them. There definitely is truth to the childhood saying, "It takes one to know one."

My third wish involves training foster parents. The horror stories shared by other foster children about their placements make me realize that Mrs. Taylor was not a monster of a foster parent. She did not harm me physically or sexually or deny me food or other material necessities. Instead, during the six years I lived under her roof, she failed to make me feel loved and emotionally secure, the things I needed most. I so very much wanted to know that she cared about me, as Dr. Folman did, but, instead, Mrs. Taylor made me feel like an unworthy burden. Perhaps if she had understood how important it was to my emotional growth to treat me with affection, rather than disdain, she may have at least tried. I do not remember her attending any seminars or training sessions. I would like to think that she was not entirely emotionally dead inside or too set in her ways to learn how to improve her foster parenting skills. It is because I believe that most foster parents want to be better guardians that I have bared my soul in this book, so they can learn from my experience and translate that knowledge into actions that benefit the children in whose care the foster care system has entrusted them.

Who Am I?

❦

Elizabeth Sutherland

Internships are steppingstones. They provide real world experiences for students transitioning from academic to professional careers. I know all about transitions. As a child, I transitioned from Spain to America and then one placement to another, never knowing stability or a sense of belonging. Then, at age 18, I transitioned from ward of the court to emancipated adult. The transition from dependent child to independent adult could have done me in, as I have seen it do to others like me, but I vowed to conquer it, to succeed, no matter what. I wanted to have a better life as an adult than I had known as a child. Really, now that I think about it, all I have ever wanted is to feel normal, like the lucky kids, the ones with parents to love and guide them.

The internship caught me by surprise that crisp February morning. I had just begun scrolling though my email when the announcement popped up on the computer screen: "Internship in Washington D.C. Deadline April 17, 2004. Apply Now." The announcement had come from the Orphan Foundation of America, the organization that had provided financial aid to me my junior and senior years of college.

Oh, my God, I thought to myself. I could barely contain my excitement, and called in my roommates. "Look at this!" I exclaimed. "I've just got to apply, don't you think?" All three girls agreed, bouncing in unison for emphasis.

I was in my final semester of college, and, I must admit, feeling a bit worn down from years of attending classes, studying into the wee hours and holding numerous jobs. I had no clue what I was going to do after graduation. I just kept my head down and worked hard to complete my undergraduate education, giving little thought to the upcoming transition from college student to adult professional. Oh, sure, I fantasized about taking a break from the merry-go-round of life to travel to some exotic place for the summer, but I did not think myself worthy of such self-indulgence. After all, I was a foster child and therefore had no sense of entitlement.

Despite struggling with self-doubt, I decided to apply for the internship. After all, I might get lucky. Miracles do happen. I figured that if I gathered all the information required to complete the application and sent it in immediately, it would improve my chances of winning. I filled out the formal application that day, but still had to forward an exemplary class essay, a list of references and a letter stating why I would like to participate in a summer internship in Washington, D.C. It took me several days to assemble everything, but the moment when everything came together, I did the unthinkable; I froze up and could not push the send button on my email.

"Why aren't you sending it in?" questioned my roommates. "You have worked too hard and come too far to quit now."

"I know, but what kind of chance would I have of winning? I'm a foster kid, an orphan, Miss Nobody," I rationalized.

My roommates refused to let me off the hook. "You have nothing to lose and everything to gain," they pointed out. "Besides, this could be your ticket to a better life. Don't blow it. Send it. Send it now."

I knew the girls were right. The worst thing that could happen was not to win the internship, a guaranteed outcome, if I did not send the required information. I choked back my fear of being unworthy of such a wonderful opportunity, dropped back down at my desk, threw my hands up in the air, took a deep breath and clicked the send button.

I majored in Business Administration and Computer Information Systems in college because information technology relates to many professions, including criminal justice, my area of interest. My ambition is to become an FBI agent in the field of Crime Scene Investigation. The internship in D.C. could help me get closer to my goal, I reasoned, if only I could win it.

As the weeks slowly ticked by, the anticipation ate away at me. I often found myself sitting before the computer, the tips of my fingers tapping nervously on the scratched wooden desk. Some days, I checked my email five or more times. "Come on. Be there," I commanded the computer, hoping that my wishes would elicit a response about the internship. I just wanted an answer, any answer, even a no answer, because I was so wrapped up in the fantasy of winning the internship. I could think of nothing else.

After nearly a month of endless wishing, praying and nail biting, I received the email. My heart dropped through my stomach, sweat flushed my pores and I began preparing myself for what surely would be bad news. Lo and behold, though, the email explained that if I were one of the top ten applicants selected, I would receive a phone call confirming my receipt of an internship. I had somehow made the cut. Now I really was nervous.

Each day seemed like a week, as I awaited final notice of the internship. "Maybe they will select me," I hoped deep in my gut. "No, not you; you're just not that lucky;" my mind prepared me for the worst, as it has always done, to shield me.

Then, after eleven days of inner-debate, the telephone rang and my roommate, Shanna, yelled from the living room, "It's a man asking for you, Elizabeth! He says it's about the internship."

I never knew the beating of my heart could be so loud or that my feet could weigh as much as they did that day. I lumbered from my bedroom along the hallway into the living room, where Shanna held the telephone in my direction, her pretty face aglow with a smile of anticipation. The phone weighed a ton, as I put it to my ear.

The voice on the other end spoke softly. "Hello Elizabeth, I am Pat from the Orphan Foundation of America. On behalf of the scholarship program, welcome to the 2004 Internship Program to Washington, D.C."

I have not a clue what I said to Pat. I suspect that I kept repeating the words, "Thank you!" but all I can truly remember is that I couldn't stop smiling, until I started crying, and then I was doing both at once. It was as if I had won a million dollars or been reunited with my birth family. My life was coming together. Maybe I could finally escape my past and start a new life, a normal life, not the life of an unwanted foster child.

The Orphan Foundation of America was the key to my success the last two years of college, providing me $2,500 per semester for tuition and books. In many ways, the Orphan Foundation supported me, much as a family would do for one of its own. More than financial aid, they provided me hope, loyalty and a sense of belonging; what happened to me actually mattered to them. The Orphan Foundation of America made it possible for me to become who I am today, and this organization continues to help other children reach beyond the limitations of not having family support.

I graduated May 8, 2004 from Western Carolina University. Three days later, I was on my way to Washington, D.C. I spent nearly two months in D. C., interning for the Siemens Corporation, where I functioned as an assistant to various executives, including the Vice President of Homeland Security.

Siemens' headquarters adjoined the FBI building. One day, when I finally mustered the courage, I filled out an application to become an FBI agent. I even had an interview. During my conversation with the FBI agent, I told him that I had grown up in placement and asked him if this would harm my chances of employment. He told me that my status as a former foster child should make no difference; however, like all applicants, I would have to pass a rigid security clearance. That is when I realized that my dream of becoming an FBI agent had less than a snowball's chance in hell of ever happening and I withdrew my application. How could someone else make sense of my past, if even I do not understand it?

All I know about my birth and early childhood is that I was born in Rota, Spain, June 9, 1980. My name is Elizabeth Sutherland. I have no middle name. All I have to identify my origin is a 3" × 5" piece of paper called a "Certificate of Birth Abroad."

I barely remember arriving in the United States, although I think I was five years old at the time and I know I did not speak English. A man named James William Sutherland escorted my brother, sister and me on the trip from Spain to America. He brought us to his mother's house in Waynesville, North Carolina one rainy evening, handed us over to her like three unwanted kittens and then disappeared forever.

My brother, sister and I arrived at Nell Dean Sutherland's trailer emaciated, covered in filth and with cigarette burns covering our bodies. Nell Dean told us that our birth mother in Spain had traded us to a street prostitute. The woman who bought us made us beg on the streets for food and burned us with cigarettes as punishment for not being good panhandlers. All three of us had deep round burn marks from head to toe. We had no clothes, except for the ones we wore, tattered rags. I remember having a potbelly that made me look pregnant at age five, probably from malnourishment. Nell Dean said we were so hungry that we tried to eat our own excrement.

The rustic tan and yellow singlewide trailer reeked of mold and mildew. We lived atop a wooded hill surrounded by other dilapidated trailers. Our singlewide had three tiny bedrooms, a kitchen, living room and one small bathroom with a washing machine tucked behind the door. Nell Dean occupied the master bedroom. Her handicapped son lived in the second bedroom. He must have had a terrible accident because he could barely speak; his fingers curled up into his hand claw-like and his eyes crossed. My brother, sister and I slept in the third bedroom, where the three of us shared a twin bed, one small closet and a single dresser drawer.

We bathed only once a week, on Sunday. We three siblings bathed together in the same bathwater Nell Dean had just used to clean herself. She refused to run fresh water for our baths or to allow us to bathe separately, "to save money," as she was quick to point out. Likewise, clothes washing occurred only on Sundays, so we wore the same filthy clothing day-after-day. The ridicule and laughter of other kids mocking my offensive body odor still haunts my memory. At one point, my teacher sat me out in the hallway because I stunk so badly. To make matters worse, Nell Dean's mangy brown Terrier peed on our clothes, but we still had to wear them until Sunday.

When I was eight, Nell Dean's daughter and newborn twin girls moved into the trailer. The responsibility of staying up at night to feed and diaper them fell to me. Also during this time, Nell Dean's parents, who lived a 30-minute cab ride away, suffered illnesses that required regular attention. For nearly three years, I had to give up my weekends to nurse Nell Dean's mother, until she passed. Nell Dean then moved her ailing father into the trailer. Nine people and one mangy dog now crowded the singlewide that could comfortably accommodate less than half that number.

That is when the physical abuse began. Nell Dean had emotionally neglected us since that rainy night her son dropped us in her lap and vanished. Never once did she hug us or say she loved us or show us affection. Instead, she chain-smoked Marlboro reds and treated us like unwelcome guests whom her son paid $300 per month to house, feed and clothe, but now, she took to beating us. I can still feel the sting of her slaps across my face, the kind that leave bright red finger marks. Neither will I ever forget the taste of my own blood caused by a metal cowboy belt buckle tearing at my nose and cheekbones, nor the shooting pain of a hickory limb leaving raised welts that itched for weeks on my back, buttocks and legs or a gut-punch that steals your breath away only seconds prior to puking. We three unwanted children became the outlet for Nell Dean's frustration, and as the walls of the singlewide closed in on her, we suffered the consequences.

Emotional neglect and physical abuse were not the only ways Nell Dean made us pay for disrupting her life. She would not allow us to associate with the other kids in the trailer park. We had to be in the trailer by 5:30 p.m. or she locked us out. We could not watch the television she kept in her bedroom, nor could we open the refrigerator without her permission. She even went so far as to padlock it on occasion. Perhaps most insidiously, there were times when she did not feed us, but when she did, she fed us the same three meals: Cheerios for breakfast, hotdogs or bologna sandwiches at lunch and pinto beans with water biscuits for supper. I kid you not. On the other hand, though, the rest of them dined well and often. Even the mangy mutt ate better than the three of us did, at least enjoying castoff pizza crusts, off-limits to us.

Everyone in the trailer park probably suspected that Nell Dean mistreated us, but because she forbade our associating with the neighbor kids and their families, no one knew for sure. I remember sneaking over to a classmate's trailer to eat with her family. Since I kept showing up begging for food, they also noticed my bruises, black eyes and welts. That is when the Department of Social Services started showing up. Nell Dean told the social worker I got that way picking blackberries, which is how we kids made money to buy clothes and school supplies. A DSS worker came to check on us nearly every week after that, but did not remove us. Frustrated by how easily Nell Dean appeased them with her lies, I sneaked over to my friend's trailer and called DSS, informing them how Nell Dean beat us and threatened to kill us by putting a gun to our heads. I told DSS that if they did not send someone out to get us, she would kill us or we would kill her.

I was 13 ½ that fateful summer day. My brother, sister and I picked away at the blackberry bushes beside the macadam road that led to the trailer park, pricking our fingers on the thorns and filling our rusty buckets, when a passing car came to a sudden stop and then backed up toward us. A woman in a neatly pressed navy blue dress and jacket and white blouse stepped out of the car and asked, "Are you Elizabeth Sutherland?" I whispered "Yes, Ma'am."

The woman smiled down at me and introduced herself. "Hi.
I am Mrs. Jenkins, and I'm from the North Carolina Department
of Social Services. I've come to take you away from here. Now come
with me, please."

We three children obediently followed her to the car and
huddled together in the backseat. My emotions ran wild as my brain
bustled with questions. Where was she taking us? What would Nell
Dean say? Should I be scared or happy? Was this really happening?
Pressed tightly together there in the backseat of the well-dressed
woman's car, we three siblings had no clue that this would be our
last time together.

Nell Dean sat at the kitchen table sipping black coffee and
puffing on a Marlboro red as we burst into the rusty trailer and
began gathering our few belongings. "What the Hell are you brats
doing?" she questioned through a haze of grey smoke.

"They're coming with me," advised Mrs. Jenkins, as she
entered the trailer and headed towards Nell Dean.

"Who are you?" Nell Dean demanded.

"I'm Mrs. Jenkins, from the North Carolina Department of
Social Services. I'm here to take custody of these children."

A heated debate between Nell Dean and Mrs. Jenkins
ensued. Nell Dean puffed away at her cigarette and demanded that
I remain with her. I'm not sure why she chose to keep me, although
I assume it had nothing to do with caring about me as a person and
everything to do with losing her slave and whipping-girl.

That is when I panicked. I cried, screamed and begged Mrs.
Jenkins to take me with her. "Don't leave me here! Please! Please!
Please take me with you! Please," I sobbed convulsively.

Nell Dean's face turned crimson and I swear smoke shot
out of her ears as she cussed away at Mrs. Jenkins. The next thing I
knew, we piled back into the car, our meager belongings resting on
our laps, and headed into the unknown. I did not so much as look
back at the decrepit trailer or utter a single word during the getaway.
I felt numb and stared straight ahead, my brain wrestling with what

had just occurred and questioning the future. Nothing could have prepared me for what happened next.

We pulled up to the DSS building in Waynesville. Mrs. Jenkins separated my brother from my sister and me, and walked him to another car. I didn't even get to hug him good-bye. The last image I have of my brother is that of his wailing, crying and struggling to reach towards me though the rear window of the car that drove him away that day, out of my life forever. His eyes, his frightened eyes, still haunt me.

Mrs. Jenkins tried to soothe my sister's and my tears by telling us that our brother was on his way to a "wonderful" foster family. Even to a naïve 13-year-old, her words smacked of betrayal. On the day that we should have rejoiced over our liberation from the cruelty of Nell Dean, we experienced only heartache and loss. Living with Nell Dean might have been Hell, but breaking up our little family truly was cruel and unusual punishment. To this day, I still do not understand the insensitive policies of a foster care system that pulls siblings apart.

Initially, my sister and I ended up at the Broy Hill Group Home, where we shared our own private bedroom. After a week, however, DSS placed us with a foster family that warehoused children. Kids slept on bunk beds, couches and the floor; anywhere they could rest their weary heads. I remember counting as many as seven kids, not including the foster parents' biological son. Foster kids came and went; some stayed a night or two; others remained a few weeks or several months; my sister and I, though, spent nearly two years there. In some ways, it was worse than living with Nell Dean.

Mr. and Mrs. Inzer were far from exemplary foster parents. In fact, they resembled prison guards more so than they did caregivers. Mrs. Inzer had the social skills of a wolverine. She showed no affection for the foster children in her charge; indeed, she seldom displayed any emotion. Mrs. Inzer zealously avoided dealing with problems or anything involving work or stress. That is probably why she spent much of the day alone in her bedroom reading magazines and watching television. She was a foster parent not for the love of children but for the love of money. What she also loved were Virginia Slim cigarettes, which she chain-smoked, and coffee, gallons of it.

Mr. and Mrs. Inzer's son, Michael, was a dirty rat. He obviously hated living with a house full of foster kids, and he took it out on us at every opportunity. He broke things and then blamed us or made up lies to get us in trouble with his parents. Michael bullied us at school too, getting his friends to call us mean names, such as "Orphan Annie" and "foster creep," or poking and shoving us at the school bus stop.

Mr. Inzer was a pig: a vile, disgusting, perverted pig. If there is a Hell, may the Devil impale him on a spit and roast him for eternity. He used to make me put on a string bikini and spread my legs so that he could look at my privates. All the while, he made grunting pig noises and licked his lips. He stared at my breasts too, not just when he made me wear the bikini, but anytime he figured nobody would catch him staring. As a 15-year-old going through a growth spurt, the more I developed physically, the more interest he took in me. I would bet my last dollar that he stalked the other girls, perhaps doing even more to them than he did to me. He was a sexual pervert whom the state of North Carolina gave a license to prey on powerless children and then failed to monitor.

DSS should have done a better job of safeguarding me from Mr. Inzer. I told my social worker about the string bikini. She did nothing about it. Then I told my next social worker about Mr. Inzer, who also dismissed my accusations. Social workers came and went. None of them took the time to know me, let alone address my concerns. They even denied my requests for a transfer. That is when I realized they really did not care about me, a worthless foster kid. Like Nell Dean and the Inzers, the DSS workers seemed to be in it for the paycheck. I finally accepted that I was on my own, with no one else on whom to rely, so I devised a plan to get myself out of there.

I'm not sure how I came up with the idea to act crazy. I began hiding under my bed, sobbing and pretending to hear voices in my head. Suddenly, I gained everybody's attention: the Inzers, my current social worker, the whole system. That's when I learned a valuable lesson about being in placement: you have to act out to get attention. Nobody heard my voice as a quiet, shy girl, but everybody certainly took notice when my behaviors screamed for help. I guess the squeaky wheel really does get the grease. The next day, my social worker drove me to a psychiatric hospital.

I continued acting oddly, though gradually less so, for six weeks. I actually liked living at the psychiatric hospital. The doctors, nurses and staff made me feel that they cared about me. Somebody was always asking how I felt, did I need anything or just checking up on me, not like the foster care system that pretty much ignored me. Although surrounded by crazy people, I felt safer at the psychiatric hospital than I did in the care of the Inzers. My therapist attended to me as if I actually mattered, not as if I were a lowly mental patient or worthless foster kid. She listened to what I had to say and offered me what she called "food for thought," insights and observations to ponder. It was almost like having a mother or a father to help me understand how to deal with problems. No adult had ever taken the time to treat me as though my life had value. Instead, adults had made me feel like less than nothing, a worthless burden they were doing a favor to keep alive. As soon as I got comfortable there, my psychiatric evaluation ended with a diagnosis of "acute depression" and I returned to the custody of the Inzers.

Less than a week after my return to foster care, Mr. Inzer resumed his perverted piggery. I knew I had to get out of there and began acting out again. I returned to the psychiatric hospital for another six weeks of evaluation. I think my therapist finally put two-and-two together and realized that I was acting out to get away from Mr. Inzer, and advised the authorities that a transfer was in my best psychological interest. The only sadness I felt about leaving there was that this time I waved good-bye to my baby sister whom, despite my requests that we remain together, DSS refused to transfer with me.

DSS decided that I should go to a therapeutic foster home because I needed individual attention. They parked me at the Crossnore Group Home for about two months and then placed me with Jack and Shirley Simmonds, who lived in Murphy, North Carolina. Finally, DSS did something right for me.

Mr. and Mrs. Simmonds had raised eight children of their own. Now empty nesters in their fifties, the Simmonds' used their considerable childrearing skills to foster-parent wards of the state experiencing emotional and behavioral problems. Neither of them was a trained therapist. He was the pastor of a small church and she raised children and kept house. They were humble, God-fearing people who used commonsense and affection (plus a whole lot of religion) as the prescription for the children in their care. They took only two foster kids at a time and they treated us as if what happened to us mattered to them. I honestly think they cared more about making a difference in our lives, than they did about the money. I lived with the Simmonds' from 9th grade through my high school graduation. The three years I stayed with them did make a positive difference in my life. In my eyes, they are heroes.

DSS, however, continued to fall short. For the three years I lived with the Simmonds', I pressed, whoever was my social worker at the time, to see my brother and sister. The pat response was "someday." I saw my sister twice during those years, but never my brother. I did not know if he was dead or alive. It was almost as if DSS conspired to keep the three of us apart. That is why I was so depressed. Not only was I parentless, I no longer had access to my brother or sister, either. One at a time, I had lost all connection to family. "Who am I?" I remember asking myself those lonely years in placement. The answer remained elusive.

Four months before my 18th birthday, DSS called, stating that they needed me to take a DNA test. Why did they need to test my DNA? Was something wrong? Had they found my mother or father? Did it have to do with why I could not see my brother or sister? My depression worsened, as I worried about what the test results would reveal.

When the result of the DNA test came back, DSS informed me that James William Sutherland was not my father and that although my brother, sister and I shared the same mother, each of us had a different father. James William Sutherland fathered only my brother, Jonathan William Sutherland, but who fathered my sister, Melissa Nell Sutherland, and I remained a mystery. I guess that I had subconsciously clung to the hope that he was our biological father, and that some day he would return for his three children and reunite our family. The last remnants of my wistful foster-kid family fantasies now dashed, I sunk deeper into depression. My questioning of "Who am I?" soon found companionship in the question, "What will become of me?"

I graduated from Andrews High School June 4, 1998; turned 18 June 9th and moved into a one-bedroom apartment the next day. I had barely more than the clothes on my back when I exited placement: no furniture, no bed, no job, no friends and no adult to guide me. Depressed and disconnected, I fell in with the wrong crowd, who introduced me to alcohol and drugs. I self-medicated for a while, as I tried to fit into society. I was so scared, so confused, so alone, so traumatized by my past and so intimidated by the future. I just wanted to belong. Oh, how I needed to feel a part of something . . . anything.

I began working at Wal-Mart that summer and enrolled at Tri-County Community College in the fall. The party group and I separated. I made new friends with Wal-Mart employees of all ages and looked to the older employees for advice and guidance. At a particularly difficult time, I asked DSS for tuition assistance, food stamps, a cot at a halfway house—something. They treated me as they had prior to emancipation; like an illegitimate stepchild deserving of nothing. As always with DSS, I was on my own.

Working as many as three part-time jobs at a time, I graduated from TCCC with an Associate of Arts degree. With financial help from the Orphan Foundation of America and multiple part-time jobs, I graduated from Western Carolina University a few years later with a Baccalaureate degree in Business Administration and Computer Information Systems. The internship in Washington, D.C., sponsored by the Orphan Foundation of America, quickly followed graduation.

I still remember the pride I felt as I crossed the stage to receive my college degree, and less than a week later, I smiled so wide my face hurt, when I stood on the platform with the other interns to address the U.S. Congress. In my wildest dreams, I could not have conceived that someone like me, a lowly orphan, would receive such an honor. As the other interns responded to the question, "What one thing would you do in your state to improve the foster care system?" I could only think about how much I missed my brother and sister. Frightened as I was, I put on my best smile and told them how important it is to keep siblings together because sometimes that is the only remaining connection to family we have left. Not knowing who your biological mother and father are is already too much to handle, but then losing your siblings in the system destroys any remaining sense of belonging. I am sure I stumbled over my words some, and at one point, I couldn't see anymore, not through the tears. Men and women dressed in their Sunday best stood and clapped. Cameras flashed from all directions. The other Orphan Foundation of America interns hugged me or shook my hand; they understood my emotional answer to the question about improving foster care.

Today, I'm twenty eight years old. I work for a bank during the day and pursue a second baccalaureate degree in criminal justice at night; I have not given up on my dream to be an FBI agent. I have reconnected with my half-sister, Melissa, and the two of us visited our half-brother, Jonathan, three years ago in New York, before he moved to Alaska, to work on a fishing boat. He is a loner, probably because of his experiences in foster care. Jonathan gave me the telephone number of an aunt who lives in Holland. I called her and learned that our mother is still alive, but in ill health due to tuberculosis. The aunt did not know who fathered me, nor does anybody else. Maybe I will never know that part of who I am. What I do know, however, is that I am one of the lucky kids who survived foster care, despite the many failures of the system designed to protect me. My name is Elizabeth Sutherland, and that is what I know about myself thus far, as I try to put the broken pieces of my life together, in an attempt to understand who I am.

Pay Me Now or Pay Me Later

⁓❧⁓

Claudette Braxton

Because my earliest childhood memories have faded with the passage of time, I turned to my three siblings to help me fill in the blanks. Our combined remembrances paint a picture of a fatherless family in turmoil, perhaps explaining why I chose to forget or repress my memories of that period. A year or so prior to entering elementary school, however, my childhood memories come alive, and, with the aid of my two sisters and one brother, I clearly see myself living in the Willow Run Village on Clay Hill, a housing complex created to shelter the families migrating from the South to get jobs in the Detroit automobile factories.

I have no early childhood memories of my mother, probably because I did not live with her. Instead, we four siblings moved about between family and friends, due to my mother's absence. My oldest sister Paulette states that around her seventh birthday, which made me about two, Mother suffered the ravages of tuberculosis. In those days, persons with TB lived in special hospitals called "sanatoriums," often for years or until their death. Paulette also relates that she and my youngest sister Cathy, who was one year old at the time, went to live with relatives in Detroit. My three-year-old brother, Phillip, moved in with a male cousin we called "Uncle Sam" and I resided with a female cousin who went by the initials KD.

It is sometimes strange what you can learn if you ask the right person the right questions. As Paulette helped me fill in some of the memory gaps, I discovered that my mother remained in the sanatorium nearly two years. I was under the impression that she was in and out of the sanatorium repeatedly, because I remembered living with different family members and family friends. Paulette also shared that Cathy used to whine a lot and beg for food. This apparently got on the nerves of the Detroit relatives with whom she lived at that time, and they asked to have her removed from their care.

Shortly thereafter, Cathy and I entered our first foster home placement. I was four at the time. My memories of this placement are few, but pleasant. I remember being clean, fed and cared for, but most of all, I have fond memories of going to work with the foster mother, Mrs. Padget. She was a big woman with a big smile and an even bigger heart who worked in a hospital laundry, where Cathy and I frolicked in a sea of white bed sheets and pillowcases. After we graduated from high school, Cathy and I made a return visit to thank Mrs. Padget for taking such good care of us.

Upon Mother's release from the sanatorium, two years later, our scattered family reunited. The five of us were so happy to be back together, despite being terribly poor. Although impoverished, we were fortunate to have a network of relatives, friends and neighbors who helped us with the basics. Sadly, though, Mother became a heavy drinker, probably because of the TB, and she went on binges that lasted a week or more.

There was a predictable pattern to her drinking. The government welfare check arrived at the beginning of the month, whereupon Mother began her next bout with the bottle. Once the liquor money ran out, she went through a withdrawal process comprised of dry heaving and vomiting for at least a day and a half. Following her detoxifying, she cleaned herself up and began cooking and cleaning up a storm that would put Betty Crocker and Mr. Clean to shame. Her meals were so good that I have spent a lifetime trying to duplicate them, and she cleaned so thoroughly that you could eat off the floors. She became our mother again, the loving person who would give her last nickel to a needy stranger, not the lost woman who retreated into a bottle to escape her pain. That is what I remember most about her, that and her wisdom, which she

shared freely with us during her lucid times. She taught us about
the importance of education. She showed us how to cook and bake.
She instructed us how to sew by hand. She paid attention to our
individual interests and health issues, and she was always humming
or singing a song. She was beautiful when sober.

When Mother fell off the wagon, I assumed the role of what
the substance abuse literature refers to as the "hero," the responsible
child who takes over the household tasks and duties, while my
siblings enjoyed the freedom that usually lasted seven to ten days,
or whenever the money ran out. Her binge drinking resulted in
constant eviction notices and relocations, which forced us to move
every few months. I remember being grateful for government
commodities, including cheese, powdered eggs, powdered milk,
oatmeal, cornmeal and canned meats, such as Spam, beef and
chicken, because they provided us something to eat. We seldom had
food in the cabinets, and from time to time, we had no refrigerator
in which to store perishables. Whenever Mother was binge
drinking, we kids ate whatever we could find. When she was sober,
Mother had a God-given gift for knowing how to throw bits of this
and that together and produce sumptuous feasts.

During her binge drinking, we four children took it upon
ourselves to protect our mother. We manufactured excuses for
her absences and drunken behaviors and enabled her alcoholism
by following her commands to bum money and cigarettes from
neighbors. She also sent us to buy homemade corn whiskey from
local moonshiners who distilled their illegal brew in abandoned
buildings. Although we always complied with Mother's requests to
fetch her booze, the process of dealing with seedy men in dangerous
surroundings both scared and embarrassed us. We were even more
humiliated when we ran into her in public and she was drunk,
slurring her words, unable to balance herself, her clothes stained,
tennis shoes on the wrong feet, hair unkempt. Nonetheless, we four
siblings remained close and loved our mother deeply.

We lived like this until I was in the 7th grade. My mother
passed away of a heart attack that spring. Only Paulette was not

present that dreadful night, as she had married and moved out a few months prior. Mother, Cathy and I now shared the same bed. Phillip slept in another room. After enduring several hours of what we naively thought was loud snoring, Cathy and I awoke to hear Mother's last gasp. She died next to us, Cathy lying on one side of her and me on the other side. We shook her and cried out, "Mommy, wake up! Please wake up, Mommy!" When screaming and shaking did not produce the desired results, we prayed, "Dear God, please save Mommy." Our quivering voices blended, "Please, we beg you. We'll do anything you want, please, please!" Life had vacated her body, though, and no amount of shaking, crying, praying or bargaining could change that. Never have I experienced something so emotionally devastating. I bawled uncontrollably for days, long after there were no more tears left in me to shed.

Mother's cousin took us to live at her home while other family members made the funeral arrangements. That is when I developed a sleep phobia, probably resulting from the trauma of waking up next to my dying mother. Once the family grieved and interred Mother in her final resting place, Cathy and I went to our second foster home. Phillip moved in with Paulette and her new husband.

The foster home was only five houses from where we lived with Mother. In addition to my sister and me, the family also took in boarders. Cathy and I knew the foster parents, and Paulette and their daughter were good friends. We stayed with them until the disposition hearing. The foster parents and the boarders treated us with kindness, fed us well and made us attend church with them. We were lucky to land in their care until the disposition hearing, when our extended family stepped up to take us into their homes. Cathy and Phillip went to live with family in Detroit and I moved in with Paulette and her husband.

Kinship care may work for some foster children, but living with my five-year-older, newly married sister proved difficult for me. Paulette and her husband were married less than a year when I arrived. They were young, too, as neither of them had reached their 20th birthday. I interrupted their marriage at its beginning, and Paulette's husband let me know it. Poor Paulette, she bore the brunt of it, stuck between two types of love, the love of family and the love of romance. All communications to me from my brother-in-law came through my sister. I felt so bad that she had to listen to him complain about me. To remedy this, I stayed away as often as I could. I had a best friend who lived down the street. Her house became my second home, where I escaped to lessen the strain between Paulette and her husband. I felt more comfortable there.

Adopting a friend or family that provides asylum is a survival mechanism used by many foster kids. We need to feel safe and we crave a sense of belonging. Some of us join gangs to fill these basic human needs. I joined a family. Unfortunately, though, Paulette and her husband misinterpreted my absence as running the streets and getting into trouble with boys. Oh, sure, I attended house parties and dances, but I was not interested in getting into trouble nor did I yet like boys. I just wanted to dance and show off the matching outfits my girlfriend and I spent much of our time together creating.

While Paulette and her husband debated how I should live elsewhere, Cathy and Phillip struggled to fit in with the Detroit side of the family. Cathy describes her time in kinship care as a "hard knock life." She remembers one of the family's "real" daughters slapping her, and her catching blame for everything that went wrong in their home. She felt like an outsider, not a family member, and that no one cared about her or Phillip. To get to school, for example, they had to catch a city bus, but they received no money to pay the fare. Cathy recalls Phillip pulling her through the back window of the bus after he had sneaked on. Eventually, they grew tired of "stealing rides," as she describes it, and started skipping school. Their truancy caused the school to alert the police and our family to their nonattendance.

That is when Cathy decided that she had had enough and called our state worker to remove her from our cousin's home. She also requested that I join her. I do not remember anyone asking me for my input, but I ended up with her in our third placement, nonetheless.

This assumption by foster care professionals that it is not necessary to consult us about our placements or other important decisions happens to foster children routinely. Seldom do the people charged with our "best interests" ask us what we think is best for us. Strangers make crucial decisions that affect our lives and they just expect us to cooperate like mindless sheep. If we question or make a stink about it, we're branded conduct disordered, antisocial, rebellious or some other pejorative term because we have the moxie to stand up for what we believe is in our own best interest, not someone else's perception of what is best for us. What arrogance! How would you feel if someone who knew little or nothing about you made important decisions concerning your life without consulting you? Foster children deserve the same consideration in this matter as is accorded adults. Taking away our dignity and assuming total control over our lives usurps our sense of independence, our ability to plan and make important decisions on our own. Perhaps that is why so many of us fall on our faces when the system suddenly and without adequate preparation emancipates us on our 18th birthday and expects us to magically transition to independent adults. Such patronizing assumptions and policies are to blame for many a foster child's failed life. Just as loving parents would do for their children, foster care professionals must include foster children in determining where they live and what is to become of them by teaching them the decision-making and independence skills required for a successful emancipation experience.

My new foster home was in the country. I vividly remember giant mosquitoes, no streetlights, icy roads in winter and muddy roads in spring. A coal stove heated the home, causing coal soot to darken the walls. The drinking water reeked of sulfur, and bathing and flushing the toilet were greatly restricted. This was a radical change for kids who grew up in the city. Furthermore, the foster mother was a strict disciplinarian who could not cook, and the foster father constantly shushed us until he went to work.

The best part of placement with the DeLaine family was living with Cathy. Staying together made living in the care of strangers more bearable and helped both of us to retain our individual identities. Another good thing about living with the DeLaines' involved regular church attendance, where Cathy and I became active in the choir. We enjoyed going to church on Sunday and other church-related activities throughout the week. This was our only outlet to interact with kids our age outside of school. We also became a part of the church family and the membership embraced us. It was at church that we felt accepted for who we were, not criticized for where we had come from. Church did not belittle or criticize us; it lifted us up.

Our foster mother did judge us, however. She tried to make Cathy and I feel indebted to her for taking us in by implying that she knew things about our family of which we were not aware. It intrigued us that she had secret knowledge about our family, supposedly negative stuff we did not know, but it also angered us that this information was used to keep us in line or to make us feel that we did not have options outside of her care. At times, we even felt that our family's integrity was under attack. Her attempts to manipulate us by implying that our family had a checkered past motivated me to work hard to be a better person. Sometimes, her negative statements made me feel like my identity was at stake. I became obsessed with making sure that my foster mother could not take credit for who I was as a person, that everyone should know that I am who I am because of the time I spent with my mother and the lessons she instilled.

Foster parents should never disparage or attempt to take the place of a foster child's biological parents. Most foster kids just want fair, honest and respectful treatment, and they will reciprocate, maybe not immediately, but eventually, with trust. Manipulation, degradation and other forms of psychological abuse, however, guarantee quite the opposite response.

In contrast, a good aspect of living with the DeLaine family involved permitting us to have company at their home, once we had completed our schoolwork and chores. Especially in the summer time, young men who attended our church or lived nearby came courting. Cathy and I played board games and cards, rode horses and listened to music with them. Mrs. DeLaine kept a close watch over us and a tight rein on our behaviors. She often played with us or joined in our conversations to get to know the boys better. She would also tell the boys that if they wanted to continue visiting us, they had to attend our church. I certainly admire and thank her for such close supervision and a strict dating policy. My husband of 33 years was one of the young men who came to visit me. He willingly complied with my foster mother's rules so that he could get to know me better.

There are so many other life lessons that no one took the time to teach me in my formative years, simple but important things that mothers teach their daughters, such as feminine hygiene and the birds and bees. Moving about in the care of one stranger after another can cause foster children to miss important life lessons. Temporary caregivers often wrongly assume that the children in their care know more than they do, or they ignore this essential building block in the maturation process. Consequently, many of my life lessons resulted from trial and error or imitation of other people's behaviors. I did not have the benefit of a consistent parent or mentor to direct me. For example, I did average work in school because no one talked to me about the possibility of going to college or the importance of doing my best. Perhaps that is because no one responsible for my care had a stake in my outcome. It mattered little to them if I became a brain surgeon or a hooker, so long as I stayed out of trouble while under their supervision.

Speculation and wishfulness often take the place of adult guidance and forward thinking for foster children. For instance, Cathy and I were unable to participate in extracurricular activities because Mr. and Mrs. DeLaines would not provide us transportation to and from school. We lived 30 minutes from the nearest town, which made it difficult to do the things that other youth our age did. Consequently, we often shared our daydreams about what life would be like if our circumstances were different.

In foster care, you do a lot of daydreaming. You spend an excessive amount of time thinking about how much you miss your mother, father, siblings or other beloved family members. You curse your bad luck, the loneliness, the uncertainty and the lack of family attachment. You compare yourself to "normal" kids who have parents and all the other things you wish you had, and then you wish you were them, if only for a day. You reflect on what you do not have and what you wish you did have. You contemplate what your future will be like when you are a grownup. Daydreams are all that remain when you have no control over the everyday reality of your life.

Throughout my entire foster care experience, I can remember only two important questions that I believe made a positive difference in my life, and neither of them came from foster care professionals. The first question came from my high school English teacher, who asked me, "Have you considered going to college to become a teacher?" Her question stunned me. I remember looking at her like a deer caught in the headlights of an oncoming car. I had not given college a thought. In fact, I had given little thought to life beyond high school and foster care, other than daydreams. I did not realize that such an opportunity was available for someone like me, a backwoods foster child. College was for smart kids with rich parents. Through good fortune or the grace of God, nonetheless, I learned about the Upward Bound program, which connected me with the support I needed to prepare for higher education.

Upon entering college, I realized that I had no home to which to return. As I grew more independent and developed my own identity, the gulf between the Delaine family and me widened. Thrust into the adult world at the delicate age of 17, I had to learn how to care for myself without their help or support from the foster care system.

The second important question came as a marriage proposal from my husband of 33 years, Willie, who also grew up in foster care. It has been a wild ride growing up together, both of us wrestling with our developmental deficits and personal issues, while trying to create a "normal" family. The fact that we both grew up in placement meant that we had little personal experience with family permanence, parental role models or unconditional love that we could include in our own philosophy of family. For example, we clashed often over what we thought was the right way to raise our sons. The compass that I used to guide me would contrast what "felt" right to me with negative experiences in my upbringing that I did not want repeated in my children's lives. My husband took his childrearing cues from his foster father. Willie had wonderful foster parents, and he felt particularly fortunate that his foster father provided excellent guidance on being a man. Our main difference in childrearing involved the use of discipline. Willie believed in using punishment as discipline, while I felt it was important to discuss the issue to make sure the children understood the reason for their discipline. Perhaps most importantly, though, was the personal commitment we made to stick together through thick and thin, so that our two sons would grow up having the advantage of family stability with two loving and united parents. We kept our vows, and as a result, we have two beautiful, college educated sons of whom we are very proud, Eric and Roshard.

Sharing the experience of growing up in foster care certainly shaped the lives Willie and I chose to pursue, both personally and professionally. For example, we agreed to work hard and pull ourselves out of poverty. We knew that education was the ticket to a better life. I insisted on completing college before we married. Willie worked for General Motors his senior year in high school. Upon graduating, the Army drafted Willie and shipped him off to the service. After discharge from the military, he returned to GM and enrolled at Washtenaw Community College, where he earned his Associate of Sciences degree and became a skilled artisan. I took a position at a human services agency that provided residential care to young persons removed from their homes due to abuse or neglect.

Early in my career, I struggled with self-esteem. I had no difficulty interacting with clients, but I did not feel comfortable stating my opinions before other professionals in staff meetings. This gap in my psychological development interfered with my professional growth for about five years. Don't get me wrong, I was good at what I did and the clients benefited from the stability I provided. However, I watched program managers come and go, and all the while, I believed that I could do their job well, but did not have the confidence to apply. Then, finally, as still another program manager prepared to leave the agency, she said to me, "They don't need to look for another program manager. They have you. May I recommend you for the position?" Shocked and gratified, I did not know what to say at that moment, although, ultimately, I did say yes. The point being that although I thought I had the ability to do the job, my professional experience outpaced my psychological maturation. Perhaps this was a residual personality trait from my foster care experience of feeling inferior because of my parentless status, as it took someone else to confirm to me that I had the skills to fill the position. Self-esteem issues plague many foster children, sometimes dramatically and for a long time.

Low self-esteem again threatened to affect my professional growth three years later when, at the age of 30, I applied for the position of coordinator for three residential treatment facilities. This time, however, I took a risk and applied for the position, knowing that I did not have the required credentials, specifically a master's degree. To my surprise, the executive director told me that he was glad I had applied for the job, but imposed a condition to my career advancement: that I pursue my MSW degree. I attended the University of Michigan, where I earned my MSW, and then applied for the professional designation of LMSW C/M (licensed master social worker with a macro and clinical designation).

The next test of my self-esteem involved earning my first professional credential. Because I did not see myself as a good student, I feared that I would not do well on the exam. After three months of nail biting, inner-debate and procrastination, I finally worked up the courage to prepare for this defining test of my social work knowledge. To my surprise and great joy, I passed with flying colors and received my ACSW (Academy of Certified Social Workers) credential in 1986, at the age of 34. Nearly two decades after emancipation, I finally shed the emotional baggage of being a foster child.

During the transition from foster child to foster care professional, I have had the good fortune to experience many roles and positions. For example, as an MSW student, I received special permission to do my fieldwork practicum at my place of employment, where my project was to design and implement a specialized foster care program for our agency. After graduation, I experienced a series of promotions, including Director of Residential Programs, Director of Clinical Services, Vice President of Programs, Vice President of Community Services and Division Director. Today, I work at Eastern Michigan University as the MSW Program Coordinator and Adjunct Lecturer. In these positions, I have an opportunity to use my personal and professional experiences to teach social work students about both theory and practice.

Throughout our careers, my husband and I have embraced the mission of making life better for children in placement. It is our way of giving back. We are two of the lucky ones who have had more good than bad experiences, as clients of a foster care system that does not always treat these vulnerable young people with the sensitivity they deserve, indeed, require. For example, we have shared many a holiday with foster children in our home. Those times when families gather to reaffirm their bonds are often the worst for foster children, for whom holidays become hell days by reminding them how they differ from other children. The delicate self-esteem of foster children suffers from a multitude of such painful realizations, which take many forms and occur much too often throughout the placement experience.

In my 42 years as a client, service provider, evaluator and educator of foster care programs, I have experienced many changes in the foster care system, some positive and others not. From my viewpoint, a critical shortcoming is the failure of the government's ethical and financial commitment to develop, replicate and fund exemplary foster care programs that enhance the ability of children in care to thrive during and after placement. Funding for foster care programs certainly is not a priority for federal, state or local government, and the condition of the foster care system receives little attention until the media reports that a caregiver has molested, murdered or otherwise grievously harmed a foster child. Public outcry then dictates assembling a panel of experts to fix the problem and ensure that it does not happen again, which, unfortunately for the clients, involves only temporary measures dictated by the same panel of experts whose policies and practices failed in the first place. To make matters worse, these panels of experts practically never include someone like me, a former client of the system. The "experts" are usually politicians, professors and administrators who run the business but have never consumed the product. How, then, could they possibly know what is best for someone like me?

An oil filter business tag line states, "Pay me now or pay me later." The message is that if you try to save money by not changing the oil filter every 3,000 miles, you will eventually spend more to repair the damage to the engine. This obvious metaphor touting the long-term value of preventive maintenance translates to foster care. As long as government continues to treat foster children as third class citizens, they will grow up experiencing deficits that threaten their adult outcomes. The disproportionate number of emancipated foster children who end up homeless, on public assistance, in prison or with other problems that limit their successful integration into society is sad testament to a system whose mission is to serve the child's best interests. If government were to embrace the long-term value of preventive maintenance by identifying, replicating and funding exemplary foster care programs that enhance the ability of children in care to thrive during and after placement, the money spent on ensuring the best possible foster care experience (prevention) would dramatically increase the clients' potential to adjust successfully and to become contributing, tax-paying members of society (outcome). Failure to comprehend and implement this obvious truth costs us all, especially children who grow up in placement. Like any machine, the foster care system requires preventive maintenance. The continued failure of government to fund the foster care system properly condemns clients to living lesser lives. "Pay me now or pay me later."

It is How Children Live that Matters, Not Where Children Live

Rosalind Folman

I do not remember when my soul died, but I must have been very young. Love, security, happiness, playfulness, curiosity, hopes and dreams were not part of my early years. I seldom asked questions, discussed my thoughts or revealed my feelings because no one in my family really cared about me. They were too busy dealing with their own pathologies. I merely existed, a confused little girl who disconnected emotionally as my subconscious mind attempted to preserve my sanity.

I did not suffer the physical abuse, sexual abuse, domestic violence or abusive acts of foster parents so often associated with soul murder. Rather, the subtly destructive acts of emotional neglect and rejection, first by my parents and then other kinship caregivers, robbed me of my childhood, of any sense of joy and excitement in life. So while violence did not snuff out my spirit, the damage of emotional neglect to my psyche was every bit as devastating.

Growing up in placement today differs from my childhood experience. My time predates de-institutionalization, when orphanages dominated and foster care played only a minor role. It was also before the identification of the "battered child syndrome," prior to the debunking of Freud's theory that childhood sexual abuse was "only a fantasy," and when domestic violence was still a private family matter. Although child abuse or neglect may have occurred, it was not a reason to remove children from their homes. Instead, most children entered care due to parental death, illness, incarceration, abandonment or voluntary placement by a parent. It is within this context, after my mother suffered a stroke, that my father placed me in a children's institution.

Although my placement experience differs from the stories that precede it in this book, many of the dysfunctional family dynamics are the same. In contrast, however, I believe my placement experience challenges the popular notion of what is in "the best interest of the child." Indeed, my experience disputes the belief that institutions are bad for children and that they need to be in a "family like" environment. My time at "the Home" was the best years of my childhood. Had I remained there until high school graduation, my adult life may very well have taken a more normal path, as it did for most of my peers who stayed until they aged out. In contrast, I moved to kinship care after only a few years. My time in kinship care, which today is seen as the "savior" for foster children, was painful and destructive, illustrating that it is not *where* children live but *how* children live that matters most.

Furthermore, while physical abuse, sexual abuse and physical neglect are the three types of maltreatment most often associated with placing children in care, research confirms that emotional neglect is the most destructive form of child maltreatment. Yet, because of the insidious nature of its effects, emotional neglect rarely receives mention in interventions or training sessions. Perhaps even more importantly, overwhelmed workers unwittingly practice it in their interactions with the children, unaware of the devastating effect on the children's lives. It is on these contradictions, between what policymakers and practitioners mistakenly "believe" is essential to a child's wellbeing and what a child "actually" needs, that I hope my story sheds light.

I am getting ahead of myself, though. To understand who I am today, we must return to the beginning, to the years before I entered a children's home in New York City. The problem is I remember only snippets of my early childhood, the totality of which provides a picture neither of a family nor even of a childhood. With the exception of a few critical scenes, I barely remember living with my parents.

My grandmother told me that prior to my mother's stroke, when she was 28 and I only four, I had a wonderful family life. However, from what I remember of my father's violent temper and my mother's self-preoccupation, I suspect it was not that wonderful. Nonetheless, my world changed completely following my mother's stroke. In one terrible moment, I went from being adored to being resented, from being the center of my parents' universe to belonging nowhere on this planet and from being the golden child to being a family burden.

I recall nothing about my mother behaving motherly towards me. While I visited her every Sunday in the hospital where she lived until her death, she never attempted to parent me. My grandmother pleaded with her to show interest in me, to ask me about my life, school or friends, but my mother seemed interested only in herself.

The few childhood memories of my father are mainly of his viciously beating my brother and kicking his head into the wall. Family members tell me that I was the apple of my father's eye, but while I wish so much that I could remember those days, I cannot.

My brother is four years older than I am. I have little memory of living with him in the same house. At age six, my father sent him to live in a Yeshiva (Jewish parochial school) during the week. While he came home on weekends, we shared little in common, leaving both of us to cope alone with our own separate pain.

My family fell apart soon after my mother's stroke, and I went to live with my grandmother, until my father's first attempt to reunite us. When I returned to my parents, my mother was heavily addicted to morphine, which she took to ease her pain. My lone memory of living with them that year was the day I registered for kindergarten. There was no excitement about my starting school. In fact, since my mother was sick and my father worked constantly, they sent me to register myself. Thus began a pattern of my family leaving me to fend for myself that continued throughout my childhood.

Shortly after school began, my family came undone again. I do not know what went wrong this time, but I moved in with an aunt and uncle and started another school. My only memory of the year I stayed with them is that no one mentioned my parents nor did my parents contact me. I thought they were dead, but was too afraid to ask.

The next year I returned to live with my parents in a new home and attended still another school. As with the previous moves and the ones to come, people just picked me up and dropped me off and I, in turn, had no reactions, no sense of loss or even any confusion about moving to a new neighborhood and new school. I just did what people told me to do, like a robot.

My mother's morphine addiction worsened, and she needed a shot every two hours. At age seven, it was my job to prepare the syringe and morphine for my father to rush in from work, give her an injection and leave. It was also my duty to watch my mother for fear she might commit suicide, which she repeatedly threatened. One day when the girl in the apartment upstairs asked me to play with her, I excitedly accepted and went with her, since no one had ever invited me over before. When I returned about an hour later, the place reeked of gas. My mother had attempted suicide. This event proved a harbinger for the end of our family.

Soon after my mother's suicide attempt and only a few months of being together as a family, my father told my brother and me that he could no longer afford my mother's drugs. My mother lay in bed screaming for morphine, screaming that continued non-stop two days and two nights. I went to my room and hid under the bed, covering my ears and praying that the nightmare would end.

That night, my brother came to my room to say he was leaving because he was afraid my father would kill him. When anything went wrong, my father beat him, so my brother climbed out the window and went to my grandmother's, leaving me alone in that nuthouse on the verge of exploding. Sunday, all hell broke loose. My mother was still screaming and my father had lost all control. He brought a pile of bricks into the house and began breaking the mirrors and furniture, all the while screaming at my mother to shut up. I remained locked in my room, curled into a tight ball beneath my bed, cowering and frightened out of my mind. When my mother tried to phone for help, my father ran into her bedroom and yanked the phone from the wall. He had never hit her, but this time was different; he seemed to be going crazy, roaming the house, smashing everything in sight and screaming so loud that his voice drowned out my mother's pleas for relief. Knowing how he viciously beat my brother and fearing that he might do likewise to my mother, I ran to her bedroom. As I got to the doorway, he grabbed the phone and raised it above his head to hit her with it. Her crippled and emaciated body was now down to about 70 pounds. Terrified that he would kill her, I cried out, "Stop, you'll kill her!" He glared right through me and shouted, "One more word out of you and you're next!" Those words are the last thing I remember, until the following Friday, when my father dropped me off at a children's institution.

This event marked the end of our family, although I do not remember ever feeling that we were a family. To this day, I have no sense of family. I cannot even imagine it. I wish that I had even vague images of my mother or father hugging or kissing me or glimpses of mundane things such as sitting at the dinner table or riding in a car with them, but I do not. The sense of family, of loving parents, is so alien to my thinking that as an adult when I walked into my neighbor's apartment and she was hugging her seven-year-old son, I asked her, "Is he sick?" When she said "No," I asked, "Is he going away on a long trip?" She said, "No." She was as puzzled by my questions as I was by her behavior. I later asked my therapist to explain it to me. He said she was hugging him because he is her son and she loves him. I sat there shocked. I said, "Parents really do that?" I just could not believe it. Now I am sure that I had seen similar scenes in my family or in movies hundreds of times before. However, until that moment I must have shut them out or just forgotten them because they confronted me so painfully, with what I did not have. It was better for me not to know, not to remember. To survive, I had to shut out so many things that make life worthwhile.

A perfect example of how adept I became at repressing my emotions so early in life was the day my father dropped me off at the orphanage. It was 3 p.m., when we pulled up to The Pride of Judea, a large institution for Jewish children, my suitcase in hand. The social worker informed my father and me that I would be living in the Home until I turned 17. At 17, when I graduated from high school, I would receive a new dress and a free week living at the YWCA. I remember thinking that at seventeen I would be a big lady and able to care for myself.

Just as the social worker dutifully laid out my future, dozens of giggling children skipped through the back door and down the steps to the basement. The social worker said they were going for cookies and milk. "Can I go, too?" I asked. Not waiting for an answer, I headed toward the stairs. The social worker called out, "Aren't you going to say good bye to your father?" I turned and stared at him blankly, then dashed downstairs to the cookie line, where I awaited my turn. The girl giving out the cookies asked if I would like to be her friend. She introduced herself as Micheline. I excitedly said "Yes," never suspecting how our friendship would alter my life.

We then ran out to play in an enormous yard filled with swings, seesaws, sliding boards, basketball hoops and a ball field. I had few experiences socializing with other children, and the excitement of actually playing with kids my age, one of whom wanted to be my friend, helped me forget that my father had abandoned me to an orphanage only minutes before. As years of insecurity had taught me how to cope, I flipped off my feelings like a light switch. I did not reflect on my situation. I did not cry or act sullen. I did not strike out in anger. I did the opposite. I ran and played with the other kids as if nothing had happened. As I ran and played, I realized a small part of my soul had survived. I just needed the right setting, a stable place where I belonged. It was "the Home," as we called it.

About 200 children inhabited the Home at that time, certainly not the "family like" setting currently considered "best practice" for foster children. I resided with the midget girls, the youngest group. There were 20 to 30 of us. We slept in a large dormitory, but ate with the other kids in a giant dining room. Each group had its own long table, as might be depicted in a Dickens story.

The Home was a big institution with little love, affection or emotional support, a place where no child was special to anyone. Since I had no memory of experiencing any of these goodies before the Home, I did not miss them or even feel entitled to them. When it comes to a lack of love and affection, however, there is a critical difference between residing in a large institution and living with someone else's family, whether it be a stranger's family or one's own relatives. In the Home, we were all equal, that is we all received no love and no affection equally. When I lived with my relatives, conversely, their children got loads of affection, attention, encouragement and other forms of emotional support. I could only look on in pain. That kind of emotional pain, the kind that says you are unworthy, that you are less than, that you do not belong, that if you died nobody would weep for you, is common in foster homes and kinship care where there are birth children. For me, it was also so debilitating that I not only had to suppress it, I had to block out the images of loving relationships that gave rise to it.

Although a large and impersonal institution, the Home was much better than kinship care in even small ways, such as birthdays, at least for me. On the last day of the month, everyone who had a birthday that month stood at the dinner table, while the other children and staff sang "Happy Birthday." Then we each received a dollar. I know it sounds impersonal to get so little recognition on your birthday, but for me it was much better than kinship care. When I lived with my relatives, I excitedly announced that it was my birthday. One time I even mustered the guts to ask why I did not receive a birthday card or presents like other family members did. The reply summed up the cold, hard truth: "You're a child no one wants, so what's there to celebrate?" I never asked again, nor did I announce my birthday after that.

Hence, living at the Home was the one time in my young life that I fit in and felt I belonged. Perhaps it was that sense of belonging that enabled me to be a child for the first (and last) time and to feel like a "normal" little girl. At the Home, I always had friends with whom to play, eat and share special events. We were a family of orphans who belonged to one another because we were all otherwise alone.

The new and much welcomed feeling that I fit in and had friends extended to the public school as well. While school supplied my one constantly positive experience throughout childhood, it was only during my years in the Home that I fit in socially at school. The other students even voted me most popular kid in the class, several times. No matter where I lived, I was always the smartest student. School was the only area of my life that gave me self-esteem, the one place where I gained positive recognition. Nonetheless, neither the Home nor school was enough to permit me the luxury of hoping, dreaming and truly enjoying my childhood.

Unlike other kids in the Home who dreamt of going back to their parents, I never thought about my parents or fantasized about living with them. In fact, I never had daydreams about anything. To have daydreams, you must have hope. Hope had abandoned me before I entered the Home. I just went through the motions of living.

A few weeks after entering the Home, at my father's weekly visit, I excitedly introduced him to my new friend Micheline and to her mother. Shortly after, my father and Micheline's mother started dating, and a little while after that, they married and started another family, of which I was not a member. Instead, he adopted Micheline and brought her to live with him. He did not even have the guts to tell me himself, but left it to my counselor to deliver the news. My response: "Now I won't be able to play with Micheline anymore." My father had just traded me for my best friend and abandoned me to the Home, and there was no support or validation of what I was going through, as nobody mentioned it again. I did not cry or throw a fit or display the slightest pain. As always, I suppressed my emotions to the deepest, darkest region of my being, the dead place where I had laid rest to my soul. I just moved on, never questioning whose fault it was that I lived in an orphanage or wondering why my father rescued my friend and deserted me. I just tried to survive, never thinking, never feeling. I was a "dead child walking."

After that, my father dropped off the face of the earth. He never again called or visited me or sent a letter or a birthday card. I forgot he even existed, at least on the surface. That was the key for me. Once I left people or they left me, they were no longer part of my conscious memory. Subconsciously, however, the wounds and suppressed emotions did not go away, but to this day remain lodged in every cell of my being.

My father's abandonment did not change my behavior in the Home or at school. In fact, that year I received the award as the smartest student in the 4th grade. To reward my educational accomplishment, the director of the home personally congratulated me and gave me a dollar. Although the Home was a large institution, there was room for validating my accomplishments, in stark contrast to kinship care where none of my successes mattered. When I graduated from junior high school at the top of my class, for example, I ran up to my aunt, whom I had to beg to attend my graduation, and asked if she were proud of the awards I had won. She said, "Oh that must have been the part I slept through." Nothing I did mattered to the people to whom it should have meant the most.

The one big change following my father's betrayal was that I no longer had any visitors since none of my aunts, uncles or other blood relatives ever bothered to come. However, my brother, whom my father had also abandoned to the Home, had permission to use public transportation on his own and could take me with him to visit our mother at the hospital on Sundays. Once a year my brother and I also went for a weekend to my grandmother's home. It was so difficult for me to leave her after that once-a-year weekend. My aunt literally had to drag me from her car to get me back into the Home. Do not get me wrong, I liked the Home, but the desire to be part of a family always tugged at me, even though I never consciously thought about it. It was just there, deep down in that dark place, as were all my feelings, hopes and dreams, and sometimes I could not hold it back.

Those few hours on Sundays and that one weekend each year were the only occasions I really spent time with my brother. We rarely sought each other out in the Home. It was his delinquent behaviors, however, that became the next thing to change my life. After months of my brother's stealing from kids and staff at the Home, staff finally apprehended him stealing his counselor's wallet. As soon as the administration located my father in California, where he now resided with his new wife and daughter, they put him on a plane and shipped him west. Nobody bothered to tell me.

A few weeks later, my counselor told me that I was leaving the Home and to pack my suitcase. I had no clue why I was leaving or where I was going, just that my aunt would pick me up. I barely had time to say goodbye to my friends at the Home. I never did get to bid farewell to my classmates or teachers. Then, in what seemed like the blink of an eye, my aunt transported me from a home filled with hundreds of laughing children to a very lonely room in my grandmother's small apartment.

When I left the Home, the spark of life that ignited there died, as did the little girl who flirted with a sense of belonging. My brief childhood had ended as quickly as it had begun, this time without cookies and milk or a best friend. I immediately forgot that I had ever lived there. Perhaps it was best for me to forget that three-year reprieve because the differences between my life at the Home and living in kinship care were so stark that memories of the Home probably would have made an already bad situation worse.

While I lived primarily in my maternal grandmother's home, it was a shared guardianship with her six children.

This kinship constellation was supposedly my new family. My grandmother hoped her children would take me in and raise me as their own, but no one wanted me. In fact, they did everything they could to communicate that I was worthless, unloved, unwanted and definitely not part of their family. I still remember these hurtful words, "Even your own parents don't want you, so you should be thankful that you have a roof over your head and aren't sleeping on the street."

My family's horrible treatment of me stemmed from their feelings towards my parents. They hated my father for abandoning my mother, brother and me, not because he hurt us, but because he stuck them with the burden. They resented my mother from childhood, when they all worked to support the family during the Great Depression and she contributed nothing. In today's foster care system, the rush to place children in kinship care leads to pressuring relatives to take the children without any consideration of the relationship between the children's parents and the relatives, often leading the children to pay the price for earlier family conflicts or animosities.

My grandmother did love and care about me, but I was in such emotional pain and so needy that I could not see it until my twenties, just prior to her death. Old age and the terrible pain of crippling arthritis that she suffered put her in no condition to raise a child. Consequently, there were no rules, limits or structure and little communication, as my grandmother did not speak English, or I Yiddish. I lived more as if I were a boarder in her home, with no one to parent me, to guide me, to soothe my pain, to applaud my achievements or to provide me the affection and validation I so desperately needed.

Throughout my years of living in the Home and with relatives, nobody said they loved me or hugged or kissed me. Even at my mother's funeral, no family member put an arm around me to comfort me. I realize now that my grandmother tried to show her love in the only way she knew how, by cooking and baking my favorite foods. I needed so much more though.

It was not until the day she died, years after I moved out, that I finally heard the words I craved so desperately. My grandmother's hearing had faded to almost nothing. My uncle, her youngest child, was screaming in her ear, "It's Maxi, your baby!" In a voice barely audible, my grandmother whispered, "Rozzy is my baby." Finally, on her deathbed, I heard the words I longed to hear all those years, that I belonged to someone. She died minutes later.

The pain of living a life devoid of affection, of emotional connection, of belonging, of even mattering as a human being was so great that I mostly slept when I was not in school. Since I barely socialized in kinship care, and had no interests or hobbies, I had no reason to be awake other than to attend school, so days without school, especially summers, were a nightmare for me. I prayed that I would die in my sleep. Thoughts of dying negated the need to plan, so I never pondered what I would do when I grew up. I just figured that if I were lucky, I would not live to adulthood.

Either no one in my family knew I was severely depressed or no one cared. Either way, I did not cause problems, so like many compliant foster children I fell through the cracks. A social worker did come once to check up on me. My aunts said, "We love her as if she were our own," and "She is an important part of the family." The social worker commented to me, "You are so lucky to have such a loving family." I did not have the courage to correct my aunts' lies. However, had the social worker the common sense to interview me in private, she may have at least taken note of my despair.

Despite my family's feelings of resentment towards me, I was so lonely at my grandmother's that I spent weekends and summers at my aunts' homes because my cousins were there and I had someone with whom to talk. They also had room air conditioners, which I could enjoy in their presence, but I could not have the AC on at night in the room where I slept because, "We aren't going to pay for electricity just for you." Similarly, when they went on vacation I was sent to another relative's home because, "You don't belong to us and we aren't about to pay to take you on vacation," as often happens in foster care.

To cope, I just tried to survive each day, never thinking about tomorrow. Despite being the top student of my high school class, I had no thoughts of a career or college. When my English teacher realized I was not applying to colleges, she tried persuading me to do so by telling me that my grades could get me scholarships to Ivy League schools. I had no idea what that meant any more than I had interest in going to college, but I liked the idea of getting a scholarship so I could tell people about it and they would think I was worth something.

I did win a scholarship to Barnard College in New York City, one of the Seven Sister colleges or Ivy League for women. I was never excited about attending college. I expected it to be like high school, the one place where I mattered and where I excelled. Unfortunately, this was not to be. Barnard accepted only the best of the best students, and among them, not only was I not special, but I was, at first, a below average student who did not fit in either academically or socially. Emotionally, I was still a child and had no interest in the social life of a college student. So here too, I was an outsider. I now had lost my only safe haven, school.

Because I was so alone, depressed and unable to cope with the realities of college, I began seeing a therapist at Barnard. Realizing I needed much support, she became the mother I never had. She was always there to comfort, encourage and listen to me, while at school and on the phone, evenings and weekends. Her dedication to helping me, while enough to get me through college, fell short of fixing the damage of childhood, leaving me to enter adulthood the way many foster children do, lacking inner resources, still carrying the wounds of earlier trauma, unable to trust and connect and unfit to integrate into society successfully. However, unlike youth aging out of care, I had a college education and a place to live, but still I was not ready to enter the world on my own.

Rarely does the foster care system address the psychological needs of youth aging out of care. Yet, too often, it is these unmet emotional needs that undermine the chances of many foster care alumni succeeding, even when they are fortunate enough to get assistance in obtaining housing and an education. For me, it was the psychological obstacles, the depression, and lack of belonging and feelings of worthlessness that determined what direction my life took when I set out on my own.

I spent decades wrestling with my psychological problems, including 25 years of therapy. It was not until I began to meditate in my late thirties that my life began to turn around. Meditation brought forth repressed memories, which I worked through in therapy, enabling me to move beyond some of the debilitating effects of my traumatic childhood. I also began to remember my life in the Home and for the first time found a purpose, to help foster children. I knew then that there was a reason for my painful childhood, to use my experiences to help improve the lives of foster children. Finally feeling emotionally ready to continue my education, in mid life, I entered graduate school at the University of Michigan and earned a doctorate in psychology.

When I finished my graduate studies, I turned my attention to learning about the psychological impact of foster care on children's development. I figured that my own childhood experience in placement, combined with my training as a psychologist, gave me a unique perspective, so that perhaps in some small way I could improve the foster care experience for other children. After years of interviewing, counseling, reviewing the literature and conducting research on foster children, several themes emerged.

Most children enter foster care already traumatized. They view the world as an unstable and uncaring place where adults cannot be trusted and tend to regard themselves in negative terms, including bad, worthless, undeserving and unlovable. They also often lack the emotional resources that are necessary to develop healthy relationships, such as the ability to trust, to care and to empathize. Despite these overwhelming barriers which hamper children's ability to adapt to a family setting, foster care focuses its energy on attaining permanency, as if that alone would solve their problems, and invests relatively little in helping children to overcome their trauma and facilitating their development. If foster care professionals do not make every effort to change the way that children view the world and build up their inner strengths, these children probably will not be able to benefit from their placement experience, whether it be temporary or permanent, or transition successfully to adulthood. In other words, foster care must become a preventive measure that is not only an intervention to alleviate immediate crises, but one that could and should prevent lifelong disastrous outcomes. All else is secondary.

Unfortunately, however, the majority of training given to child welfare personnel focuses on bureaucratic paperwork rather than helping them to identify, understand and fulfill the needs of the young people whom they are meant to serve and protect. Until child welfare personnel understand how children experience foster care and become aware of what policies and procedures help or hinder their development, the system cannot effectively facilitate the long-term adjustment of these vulnerable children, which in turn, limits their potential for becoming productive members of society.

Not only does foster care fail to promote children's development, it often impedes their emotional growth, and it does so in very fundamental areas. Foremost, the foster care experience undermines children's sense of belonging. Belonging is a basic human need that when unmet prevents children from achieving a sense of self-worth. For children to develop a sense of belonging, they must feel valued, needed and important to others. In foster care, however, poor placement experiences teach children that they are not valued in the family setting, while multiple placements not only teach children that they are disposable, but the repeated disruptions in all their social networks, losing family, friends, classmates and community, lead children to feel as if they belong nowhere.

Nor does the system attempt to help foster children develop a sense of belonging in other ways, such as the creation of support groups, which work so successfully for other children who are experiencing trauma: children of divorce, children of alcoholics, children of domestic violence or children of incarcerated parents.

For foster children, who belong nowhere, who feel stigmatized and different from all other children, such groups can also provide a family or community where they belong.

Furthermore, foster care disempowers children by silencing their voices, withholding information and giving control over the most important decisions of their lives to strangers. This obvious neglect of children's human right to have some say in what is to become of them instills a sense of helplessness and dependency, which takes its toll when youth age out and try to make it on their own.

Foster care professionals must learn to listen to the voices of foster children, both present and past. We know what is in our best interest and what is not. We know what policies and procedures work for our betterment and which do not. We know what hurts us and what helps us. We know what is required to satisfy our short-term needs and improve our long-term outcomes. We know what most foster care professionals cannot know about the foster care experience because we have lived it. That fundamental lack of perspective limits the ability of the current foster care system to operate optimally and in the best interest of the child. One result of this obvious oversight is a foster care system that its clients condemn because its policies and procedures never comprehended or addressed their psychological needs. If foster care were a business rather than a government subsidy, it would be bankrupt. However, despite the obvious, it limps inadequately on, harming more children all the while.

Finally, one major theme came to the fore, both in my life and in the lives of the hundreds of children whom I have interviewed: It is *how* children live that matters, not *where* children live. The best example of this is an overlooked and underestimated group of foster children who thrive <u>because</u> of their placement experience, children who grew up in institutions, such as children's homes and orphanages. Because of the misguided emphasis on "where" children live, as opposed to "how" they live, policymakers and politicians largely eliminated these institutions in favor of foster care. They mistakenly believed that foster care would provide children the next best thing to the nuclear family. The stories in this book and in the general literature demonstrate that for the majority of foster children, this approach failed decades ago.

Conversely, my story and the stories of hundreds of others who grew up in institutions portray a much more positive picture of life in an orphanage and the outcomes of the children who lived there. An informal survey of over 200 children who aged out of The Pride of Judea, where I lived, found that none of the residents were ever involved with the law, all graduated from high school, most graduated from college and many went on to graduate and professional schools (Craft & Friedland, 1998).

Still another survey of 1,000 former orphans conducted by Dr. Richard McKenzie, who grew up in an orphanage, found that they surpassed the national norms in all areas, including education, employment, income and satisfaction with life. In his book *The Home*, Dr. McKenzie (1996) found that only 3% of his orphanage's survey respondents had been on public assistance and less than 1% had been in prison. These findings are in sharp contrast to the abysmal statistics of children in foster care.

For example, a recent study by Fowler and Toro (2006) found that among 268 recently emancipated foster care alumni, 49% experienced homelessness; only 41% graduated from high school; 48% received public assistance; and 70% lived below the poverty level. On average, these youth were unemployed 48% of the time since leaving care; 33% had significant mental health problems; 27% were imprisoned on average 8 months; 33% were substance abusers; and 48% became pregnant or their partner did. Costs accumulated by this sample over an average of *only 3.6 years* since leaving foster care amounted to $1.0 million in public assistance, $1.6 million spent on prisons and jails and $3.7 million in lost wages compared to working full time at minimum wage.

Obviously, providing a family setting "at any cost" has proven detrimental to the lives of children in state care and has done so at an enormous cost to taxpayers. Furthermore, when adults who as children lived in foster care before entering the Pride of Judea compared their experiences, they told stories similar to those in this book and how moving to the Home saved their lives. Likewise, when McKenzie's respondents compared their foster care and orphanage experiences, 92% said they preferred living in an orphanage, compared to only 2% who chose foster care. When asked to choose between living in an orphanage and living with relatives, 75% of McKenzie's group chose an institution and only 16% chose relatives.

These findings and the stories in this book highlight our need to listen to the consumer, and we consumers of foster care, past and present, cry out: It is *how* children live that matters not *where* children live!

References
Craft, P. & Friedland, S. (1998). *An Orphan Has Many Parents*, Hoboken, NJ: KATV Publishing House, Inc.

Fowler, P. & Toro, P. A. (2006). *Youth Aging Out of Foster Care in Southeast Michigan: A Follow-up Study.* Wayne State University: Unpublished Report.

McKenzie, R. (1996). *The Home: A Memoir of Growing Up in an Orphanage*, New York, NY: Basic Books

Epilogue

Adhering to a set of developmental principles on behalf of young people growing up in out-of-home care was not the intent of this book, but insights and recommendations embedded within the reflections of the 11 authors do provide compelling and unique insight in that direction. For instance, the negative effects of multiple placements rings as clearly as a church bell in many of the personal histories, but as powerful and logical as this truth would seem, children continue to suffer unnecessarily from the instability of having to adjust to multiple unfamiliar settings. Sometimes they remain only in the foster care system, while other times they move into the juvenile justice and mental health systems too, perhaps experiencing double-digit placements. The cardboard box and plastic trash bag depicted on the cover of this book symbolize the plight of these disenfranchised children who seldom have even a suitcase in which to transport their meager belongings from one placement to the next or into the adult world at emancipation. Where is the dignity?

Talk about causing developmental issues! Consider the emotional trauma you might have suffered had you been abruptly separated from your family in childhood and then moved about in the care of one stranger after another until, eventually, you came to believe that the reason you do not "belong" is because you are worthless and unlovable. Now imagine what it is like to carry that psychological burden into adulthood and perhaps to the grave. If you read the authors' chapters carefully, you see that even though they have transitioned to adulthood "successfully," the childhood trauma of feeling unattached, unwanted and unimportant remains. Belonging is essential for healthy human development just as surely as instability promotes dysfunction.

Trust is another issue that threatens the well-being of children growing up in out-of-home care. Disconnected from loved ones and given little or no say over what happens to them, these young people develop defense mechanisms to guard their emotions and protect themselves from a system of caregivers that does not always treat them as loving parents would. Instead, too many of these children and adolescents become victims of the adults entrusted with their care. As the authors reveal in their painful recollections, physical, sexual and emotional abuse occur far too frequently in placement, although they are seldom reported to or detected by caseworkers, with emotional abuse and neglect being the most frequent and psychologically damaging offenses committed against these impressionable young people.

One would think that systems charged with the responsibility of serving and protecting our most vulnerable citizens would put being acutely sensitive and responsive to the needs of the young people at the forefront of its mission. This is not so, as the authors repeatedly state. They tell about how seldom they saw their caseworkers and how frequently they changed caseworkers. They reveal that even when they mustered the courage to talk to caseworkers about serious problems with caregivers, nothing happened. They discuss the absurdity of conducting interviews in the presence of caregivers and expecting victims to expose abuse, maltreatment or other problems they have with the people responsible for their welfare. Danita Echols disclosed how the foster care system emphasizes completing bureaucratic paperwork over conducting social work with the children in its care. A system not in tune with its mission does not inspire trust in its clients.

Neither are these young people prepared adequately for independence. After years of relying on strangers to supply nearly everything and to make the majority of important decisions about their lives and welfare, the system emancipates them at the tender age of 18. Already traumatized by the problems that required removal from their families, and then further distressed by a system insensitive to their emotional needs, these confused young people must now magically adopt the ways of mature adults and integrate into society successfully. This is a sequence of events doomed to undermine healthy adult outcomes.

Only a poor and unprepared parent fails to teach the children decision-making and independent living skills, forces them out the door before they are adequately prepared and ceases to support them thereafter. The government and its systems of care are indeed poor parents, and vulnerable young people must endure the consequences. That is why so many foster youths exit the child welfare system unprepared to succeed, only to suffer disproportionately high rates of adjustment problems, such as poverty, imprisonment, homelessness, pregnancy, prostitution, substance abuse and premature death. This certainly is not how a loving parent serves the best interests of the child. If it were, the adult outcomes of these former foster children would approximate those of children in the general population. Sadly, however, the social and emotional deficits they experienced in the care of strangers, followed by the trauma of suddenly becoming autonomous adults, a role for which they have been ill-prepared, does not readily inspire positive outcomes.

The government invokes the doctrine of *parens patriae* when it acts on behalf of a child. In theory, the state takes over the parental role and makes the protection of the best interests of the child the first and most important concern of the court, but in practice, nobody has yet designed a system of care that delivers the services required to accomplish this lofty goal. Instead, too many boys and girls still experience unsafe placements and leave care just as damaged and at risk as when the court determined it was in their best interests to safeguard them by assuming the role of the parent. As the authors reveal, most of them managed to grow past their childhood experiences in spite of the system of care that took over the legal role as their parent. How they managed to do so while others do not remains a question desperately in search of an answer.

This does not mean that the authors blame the government for intervening in their lives nor does it suggest that their childhood experiences or adult outcomes would have been better had they remained in the care of their parents or other family members. To the contrary, the authors realize that intervention may have saved them from suffering worse experiences in their family homes than they did in the care of strangers. For example, although the foster care system values kinship care as a preferred placement option, not one of the authors had a good experience in the care of relatives. As Angelique Day advises, "Kinship care homes must receive the same careful monitoring and the same resources as non-kinship homes, if we are to ensure the safety and success of children and youth placed in relative care."

No, it is not the doctrine of *parens patriae* with which the authors take exception, it is the difference between what this guiding principle promises to do on behalf of children and the reality of what actually happens to them. An aphorism states: "The road to Hell is paved with good intentions." With respect to children who grow up in the care of the state, good intentions that lack follow-through pave the way to Hell for far too many of them. They deserve a system where the policies, programs and people entrusted with their care treat them as well as would loving parents who are caring for their own offspring. That is the *raison d'etre* for *parens patriae*, its "soul" purpose.

The authors believe that most professionals who work with children strive each day to make a positive difference. They certainly do not do it for money or praise. Social work is not about self. It is about others, and anyone who works with youth and does not know this intuitively should pursue another career. The authors also believe that dedicated foster care, juvenile justice and mental health professionals want to know how to do their jobs well. That is why the authors contributed to this book, to compare and contrast their lifetimes of personal experiences and professional expertise and offer them as reference.

The authors know there is no magic pill or simple solution to optimizing services and outcomes for children and adolescents in out-of-home care, but they also believe that accomplishing this worthy goal is achievable. That is why they continue to work with or on behalf of youth in placement and why they risk baring their souls in this book. They somehow managed to survive difficult odds before, during and even after placement and go on to lead relatively normal lives. They want to pass on what they have learned. It is how they can help to improve the services to and outcomes of youth in out-of-home care.

Other former clients want to contribute, too. Many of them already work with or on behalf of children. Others work in different professions but want to help make a better life for young people growing up in care. The problem is that this rich resource remains largely untapped. Logic dictates that to know how to improve a product, one should solicit feedback and recommendations from consumers and then adjust the product accordingly. This does not happen in the foster care, juvenile justice and mental health systems. Rather, as John Seita learned by surveying 104 private Michigan child welfare agencies, only six of the responding agencies reported having board members who were child welfare alumni, and no agencies reported having either a chief executive officer or any executive staff who were child welfare alumni (Seita, 2004). One would suspect this is also true nationally for not only foster care but for juvenile justice and children's mental health services as well. Several authors decried this obvious omission of client experience in the decision-making process at the policy-making and program administration levels. They ruminated about how people who have not walked in their shoes can possibly know what is in their best interest. This is akin to a man describing menstrual cramps to a woman or a trust fund millionaire telling homeless people how to pull themselves up by the bootstraps. Talk about condescension! There is no substitute for the perspective gained by actually experiencing an event.

Additionally, youth in care require role models. They need to know that others have experienced childhoods as bad as or worse than they did, and that they went on to become productive members of society. Finally, they need to learn from them how they did it. Reading the personal histories in this book is one way to identify role models and learn from their experiences. Including former clients on advisory boards and boards of directors and in the decision-making process at the policy-making and program administration levels offers another way to reinforce the message that children no different from them have succeeded and so can they. Encouraging former clients to work directly with youth at risk affords the optimal approach because current clients can learn directly from role models with whom they share common experiences. To quote Meloney Barney, "When I met Dr. Folman, however, who was a former foster child, not a therapist; I opened up like a flower at dawn. She was so like me. She so understood me. She knew my pain and confusion." Kids need role models, especially children and adolescents burdened with the misfortune of having incompetent or troubled parents or no father or mother at all. Who better to help counter the deficit than someone who has shared the child's experience and thereby inspires his or her trust?

The mental health issues children and adolescents in placement endure are many, varied and insidious. Psychological problems are why they act out in care, why they falter upon emancipation and why they suffer emotional and behavioral disorders in adulthood. The family problems that required loss of parental custody or the trauma of losing their parents, coupled with the stressors they endured while in care, created an ideal formula for post-traumatic stress disorder. Too much stress for too long creates distress, and prolonged distress eventually short-circuits the brain.

The repetition of this theme in the authors' stories bespeaks its importance. That is why Rosalind Folman recommends that every child should have at least one weekly session with a therapist especially trained in working with traumatized children for the duration of her or his placement experience, and after emancipation, if needed. Moreover, retain the same therapist throughout, if possible. Diagnosing emotional disturbances requires consistency and the time to build rapport and trust. Undiagnosed psychological problems threaten the current and future state-of-mind of youth in placement. Conversely, early diagnosis and appropriate treatment is the elixir for most healthcare issues. Thus the proverb, "An ounce of prevention is worth a pound of cure."

Furthermore, the parenting literature emphasizes the importance of consistency in raising healthy children. Why would this not also be true for youth parented by the state? Constantly having to adjust to new placements, new caregivers, new caseworkers, new schools and other new people and circumstances can produce inconsistencies that affect the child's development. The authors note the significance stability played in their placement experiences and outcomes. For example, Waln Brown credits his turnaround to the 18 months he spent in a juvenile reformatory and Claudette Braxton reveals the value of keeping siblings together in foster care. Several authors report how school or church helped them to maintain balance while they struggled with the vicissitudes of out-of-home care. Placing them in a safe and stable environment where they can flourish may be the most important and fundamental service these young people require. As the authors' personal histories reveal, the foster care system seldom provides either safety or stability.

Perhaps that is why the title of Rosalind Folman's chapter rings so true: "It is how children live that matters, not where children live!" Rosalind describes how her three years in the "Home" represent the best of her placement experiences and kinship care the worst. She then cites a recent study that quantifies the dismal adult outcomes of foster children and discusses two books whose authors grew up in orphanages and surveyed the alumni, both survey groups experiencing exemplary adult outcomes and lauding institutional care over foster care. Rosalind's perceptive title succinctly describes why many former foster children glorify orphanages and vilify foster care.

The authors do not propose entirely scrapping foster care in favor of institutions; but they do recommend taking a closer look at model orphanages, children's homes and group homes as alternatives ways to provide children in out-of-home care the safety and stability required to enhance their placement experiences and adult outcomes.

The authors do strongly suggest improving the foster care system, however. Precisely what they would do to ensure the safety and stability and enhance the placement experiences and adult outcomes of youth growing up in foster care is a complicated subject requiring separate commentary. As the authors note in their chapters, some of their foster care experiences and placements were positive and others were not. Exploring common themes that differentiate poor practices from best practices, delineating the subtleties and proposing alternative policies and procedures deserves more thought and research than a cursory examination permits here.

What the authors do recognize intuitively is that until the government and its systems of care know what placement experiences work best for whom and why, the children and adolescents entrusted to their care will not benefit from the safety and stability that loving parents provide their daughters and sons: the minimum standard of care for which they strive. The authors have offered their experiences, insights and recommendations as a beginning point. They hope others who share their sentiments will echo their cries.

Growing up is a tough enough experience by itself. Doing so in the care of strangers is doubly so, as is unsupported emancipation. Children and adolescents, whom the court deems it is in their best interests to remove from the family home and place in the care of strangers, should not suffer for want of appropriate treatment during or support after the placement experience because of their status as wards of the state. Indeed, the doctrine of *parens patriae* demands providing the "best" services and ensuring the "best" outcomes for its clients. Anything less reinforces the trauma these vulnerable young people endured prior to intervention, thereby further handicapping them and limiting their life-long potential.

In the mathematics of social work, negative placement experiences do not promote positive outcomes. Isn't it time to recalculate what truly is "in the best interests of the child" and develop model programs, policies and procedures that enhance the placement experiences and adult outcomes of young people who grow up in the care of strangers? More specifically, how will you apply the insights and recommendations provided by the authors to improve the child welfare system and the lives of the young people who rely on your best efforts to ensure the safety and stability required for their positive placement experiences and healthy adult outcomes?

References
Seita, J. (2004). *Strength-Based Approaches Expand into Leadership. Reclaiming Children and Youth, Volume 13, Number 1, 22-25.*

About the Authors

Dr. Waln Brown, Founder & CEO of the William Gladden Foundation, spent his adolescence in a series of out-of-home placements, including an orphanage, juvenile detention facility, state psychiatric hospital and reform school. A special education student who failed the 9th grade and graduated 187th in a class of 192 students, Waln earned his Ph.D. at the University of Pennsylvania. He has authored over 230 publications, including the books *The Other Side of Delinquency* (Rutgers University Press), *The Abandonment of Delinquent Behavior: Promoting the Turnaround* (Praeger Publishers) and *Why Some Children Succeed Despite the Odds* (Praeger Publishers). Prior to founding the William Gladden Foundation in 1983, Waln held positions with the Pennsylvania Department of Education, the National Center for Juvenile Justice and the Sonia Shenkman Orthogenic School at the University of Chicago. Dr. Brown marries his personal experience of growing up in multiple placements and overcoming a difficult childhood with decades of researching and writing about the recovery process.

Dr. John Seita understands the challenges facing disconnected young people. Academically challenged students and youth who are in out of home settings, such as foster care, residential care and group care are his specialty. John is a former youth at risk who beat the odds. The court removed John from his mother's home at eight and he spent the remainder of his youth in multiple foster homes, detention facilities, group care settings and on the streets. Abused and neglected as a child, his journey though children's institutions and countless foster homes was a litany of degradation and humiliation. Few trainers and speakers have lived in the dependent care system and now share both their insiders view linked with the latest research in positive youth development, resilience, strength-based approaches and brain research. Because of Dr. Seita's advocacy on behalf of foster children, his alma mater, Western Michigan University, recently developed the John Seita Scholarship to help undergraduate students who have aged out of foster care pursue their educational goals *www.wmich.edu/fyit/ scholarship.html.* In 2007, John received the Ruth Massing Foster Care Alumni of the year award through Casey Family Programs. He is the author of *In Whose Best Interest?, God is in the Kitchen, Kids Who Outwit Adults* and dozens of scholarly articles about foster care.

DR. PHIL QUINN was born out of the union of a Native American soldier and British mother in the aftermath of World War II. Phil entered foster care at age five and experienced multiple group and individual placements until adopted at the age of eleven. For the next six years, Phil suffered severe physical, emotional and sexual abuse from his adoptive parents, until they kicked him out at age seventeen and told him never to return. He survived on the streets alone until rescued by a biker club. Faced with the prospects of life imprisonment or an early death, he escaped the bikers and pursued an education, earning a doctorate from Vanderbilt University. Dr. Quinn is founder, and until recently, CEO of ICARE, a nonprofit organization focusing on child abuse and foster care issues. In addition to keynoting and presenting at hundreds of child welfare conferences, he has appeared on numerous radio and television talk shows and authored six books with Abingdon Press, including *Cry Out!, Renegade Saint, From Victim to Victory, The Well-Adjusted Child, The Golden Rule of Parenting* and *Spare the Rod.*

ANGELIQUE DAY, MSW. Removed from her mother's home at the age of 12 for neglect, Angelique spent more than a year in out-of home care before reunification with her father. Angelique divides her time between a half-time appointment as a research specialist at Michigan State University and as a policy and outreach associate at Michigan's Children, a private, nonprofit children's advocacy organization. Prior to working in her current positions, she worked for the Michigan Department of Human Services as a child protective services worker. Mrs. Day has published in the areas of mentoring at-risk youth and kinship care. Additional research interests include issues that impact youth in transition and issues that affect American Indian families and communities. Angelique currently serves as a member of the Michigan Statewide Interdepartmental Task Force on Permanency for Youth in Transition.

DANITA ECHOLS, MSW, experienced multiple placements in foster homes, group homes and a juvenile detention facility. During her eleven-year odyssey in the foster care system, Danita attended a dozen public schools before graduation. Prior to and between placements, her dysfunctional family life consisted of abject poverty, neglect, physical abuse, emotional abuse and domestic violence. Adult family members and foster caregivers told Danita that she would "never amount to anything." Their disparaging remarks seemed prophetic, as Danita struggled to adapt to her newly found freedoms, lack of support and guidance following emancipation. Through hard work, determination and the support of people who "believed" in her, Danita earned BSW and MSW degrees. Her first professional position was as a social worker in the Philadelphia, Pennsylvania foster care system. For the past 12 years, Danita has combined her personal experiences as a client of the foster care system with her social work education and professional expertise as a foster care worker to help youth transition out of foster care. She shares her knowledge with the Michigan legislature, community panels, faith based groups and foster care organizations regarding the services required for both youth currently in care and those aging out. Danita also works with the courts, the mental health system and support groups within the same system that once parented her, the Michigan Department of Human Services.

MAURICE WEBB, BSW, is a former foster child who experienced poverty, homelessness, starvation, domestic violence, physical abuse and depression. Maurice spent his adolescence in three foster homes, a group home and even jail as a delinquent. He aged out and was once again homeless after funding stopped at age 18. Maurice worked his way through college, and with the financial help of the prestigious William Tilton Award, earned a baccalaureate degree in social work. He then combined his childhood experience with his education and professional expertise to work on behalf of foster children. Today, Maurice is an ordained minister who consults with child welfare agencies as a staff trainer and program technical assistant.

DR. DEBRAHA WATSON became an orphan, with the loss of her mother at the age of seven. Separated from her siblings and reared in several foster homes in Detroit, Michigan, she experienced physical, sexual and emotional abuse. As an adult, Debraha admits to having to pass through several stages to recover from the events of her childhood, a journey that continues to be a "work in progress." Survival and coping skills became essential as she developed along the way. Oftentimes difficult, the recovery process and the road to a healthy resolution of an abusive childhood involved intense self-reflection and painful recollection of past events and people. Dr. Watson is the Vice Chancellor of Educational Affairs/Provost of the Northwest Campus at Wayne County Community College District. She lectures at community-based organizations, hospitals, churches, colleges, foster care agencies and transitional housing on her experiences growing up in the foster care system, characterizing the psychological and emotional realities that resulted. Dr. Watson has developed workshops related to the topic of overcoming adversity and childhood abuse. She uses her personal experiences to examine why and how children fall through the grasp of society within a system designed to provide foster children and abused and neglected children with safety, permanency and well-being. Debraha uses her knowledge about social and political reform to assist those in society who have suffered abuse by fighting to change laws, policies and practices.

Meloney Barney, B.A., is a former "Ward of the State" that seemed destined to repeat the family tradition of failure. It was not unusual to lose custody of children within Meloney's bloodline, beginning with her great grandmother, who was the first to forfeit parental rights, followed by her grandmother, whose daughter, Meloney's mother, would later repeat the act. Prior to Meloney's placement in foster care, she suffered through years of domestic violence and abuse. Her stepfather and mother devoted their time to drugs and running from drug dealers for unpaid debts. For a year, drug dealers used the family home to conduct illegal business. At the age of ten, Meloney's stepfather allowed the drug dealers to abuse her sexually in exchange for drugs. Once removed from her mother's custody, Meloney experienced multiple placements and years of emotional abuse. Education became Meloney's lifeline. Inducted into the National Honor Society, she graduated from high school summa cum laude and then earned her undergraduate degree from Wayne State University. Today, Meloney is married, with two beautiful children, and aspiring to become a special education teacher. She continues to pursue a master's degree in Elementary English Language Arts while focusing on obtaining an endorsement in Emotionally Impaired Special Education. Ultimately, Meloney intends to pursue a doctorate in Rehabilitation Counseling and establish a rehabilitation youth resource unit for children in and transitioning from foster care.

Elizabeth Sutherland, B.S., was born in Rota, Spain, where her mother traded her and her two siblings to a street prostitute who turned the three children into panhandlers and burned them with cigarettes. At age five, a man who Elizabeth mistakenly believed was her biological father brought the siblings to the United States, deposited them in the care of his mother and disappeared forever. For the next seven years, Elizabeth, her brother and sister lived in an overcrowded singlewide trailer with an abusive grandmother. At age 12, the North Carolina Department of Social Services placed Elizabeth and her siblings in foster care. Elizabeth lost touch with her brother and sister as she moved from one foster home to another, during which time she suffered emotional, physical and sexual abuse. She purposely acted out until DSS moved her to a foster placement at age 15 where she received the care she needed to flourish. Elizabeth earned her B.S. in Business Administration and Computer Information Systems from Western Carolina University. She is currently pursuing a B.A. in Criminal Justice from Western Carolina University and works in banking. Elizabeth remains active in helping foster children by speaking to potential adoptive parents and foster parents.

CLAUDETTE BRAXTON, LMSW C/M, ACSW, spent her formative years living in various kinship/fictive kinship placements and in numerous foster homes before graduating from high school and earning her undergraduate degree at Eastern Michigan University and Masters of Social Work at the University of Michigan. For the past eight years, she has worked at the Eastern Michigan University School of Social Work as the MSW Program/Field Coordinator and Adjunct Lecturer. Prior to her current position, Claudette worked 26 years at human services agencies in direct practice, supervision and management positions. In her spare time, she is a consultant to human service agencies seeking to increase their capacity to service their communities. Mrs. Braxton also provides group home training to the local county services agency and participates on the local school board and several community/advisory boards. She volunteers nationally as a team leader and peer reviewer for the Council on Accreditation. Claudette has served on the board of the Michigan Chapter of the National Association of Social Workers since 2005.

DR. ROSALIND FOLMAN entered out-of-home care prior to de-institutionalization, when orphanages were the primary placement. After repeatedly being shunted back and forth between her parents' and relatives' homes, Dr. Folman, at age seven, entered an institution for children, where she was relatively happy and secure for about three years. She then went to various kinship care homes, which, unlike the institution, were places of rejection and emotional neglect. The negative effects of these placements handicapped her development throughout childhood and into adulthood. Nevertheless, she earned a B.A. from Barnard College and a doctorate from the University of Michigan. As a psychologist, Dr. Folman has worked in child welfare as a researcher, evaluator, consultant, therapist and national speaker on the psychological issues of children in care. Her research focus is the psychological development of foster children. She emphasizes the critical importance of listening to foster children's voices to learn how they understand and cope with their situation and advocates using this information to develop policy and programs.

Based on feedback from foster children, Dr. Folman has given keynote presentations throughout the country to child welfare personnel, judges, lawyers, educators, program developers and policy makers. She has also consulted with agency personnel on practices that lessen the trauma of foster care placement and facilitate children's development. Currently, she is seeking funding and collaborators to realize her vision of creating "A Place to Belong," a unique program designed to assist foster children in overcoming their adversities.

Conferences, Seminars, Speakers, Trainers, Consultants & Program Evaluators

Child welfare agencies, organizations and services providers searching for ways to train and motivate staff, conduct educational seminars, coordinate conferences, develop appropriate programs, policies and procedures or have their programs evaluated need look no further. The William Gladden Foundation and its diverse list of former child welfare clients have the expertise to help you improve the services to and the outcomes of the young people you serve. The 11 authors in this book represent personal experience and professional expertise in:

- ☐ Foster care
- ☐ Juvenile delinquency and juvenile justice
- ☐ Mental health
- ☐ Adoption
- ☐ Orphanage, institutional & group home
- ☐ Child Abuse & neglect

Learn more about our personnel, services, scheduling, honorariums and related information at:

www.williamgladdenfoundation.org

William Gladden Foundation
2804 Cavan Drive
Tallahassee, FL 32309
Phone: (850) 668-8574
Email: walnbrown@comcast.net

BOOK ORDER FORM INFORMATION

Thank you for your interest in the book *Growing Up in the Care of Strangers*. This book is available as follows:

Single or multiple copies can be ordered through the

> William Gladden Foundation
> 2804 Cavan Drive
> Tallahassee, FL 32309

Telephone orders: Call (850) 668-8574.

Email orders: orders@williamgladdenfoundation.org

Pricing: 1 to 2 books $27.95 each
                3 to 5 books $23.95 each
                6 to 10 books $19.95 each
                11+ books $15.95 each

Shipping U.S.: $4.00 for the first book and $2.00 for each additional book **International:** $9.00 for the first book and $5.00 for each additional book (estimate)

Special U.S. Offer: Send a $50.00 tax-deductible check to the William Gladden Foundation and receive a personalized copy of *Growing Up in the Care of Strangers* signed by Dr. Waln Brown (includes shipping and sales tax, if applicable).

Name: _____

Address: _____

_____

City: _____ State: _____ Zip: _____

Telephone: _____

Email address: _____